AF553781

WORKERS EDUCATION

WORKERS EDUCATION

By

Dr. Yerroju Bhaskaracharyulu, *Ph.D.*

Associate Professor
Dept. of Adult & Continuing Education
Andhra University
Visakhapatnam
Andhra Pradesh

DISCOVERY PUBLISHING HOUSE
NEW DELHI-110002

First Published-2004
Reprinted: 2013
ISBN 81-7141-886-4

Published by

DISCOVERY PUBLISHING HOUSE
4831/24, Ansari Road, Prahlad Street,
Darya Ganj, New Delhi-110002 (India)
Phone: 23279245 • Fax: 91-11-23253475
E-mail:dphtemp@indiatimes.com

Printed at:

Dynamic printers, Delhi

I Humbly Dedicate

This Work To My

Revered Parents

LATE SRI 'VIDYARANYA' MADHAVACHARYA

And

LATE SMT. VENKATA SUBBAMMA

CONTENTS

PREFACE

India, after independence, in order to develop its economy at a faster rate and to achieve self-reliance, increased its investments on the industrial sector. However, Productivity was often clouded with the problems in Industrial Relations mainly due to the fact of illiterate and uneducated work force. Thus, the Government began to seriously plan Workers' Education during the later half of the 1950s and established the Central Board for Workers' Education in 1958.

The Central Board for Workers' Education has designed several programmes, all aimed at developing an educated work force. One of the important programmes of the Central Board for Workers' Education is training of workers by their colleagues who are trained as Worker Teachers. The trade unions will arrange to organise the programmes for which the grants-in-aid will be provided by the Central Board for Workers' Education, while concerned managements are supposed to provide facilities.

The book comprehensively deals with the aspects of Workers' Education in Public and Private sectors by presenting a data pertaining to the study. This work is considered to be very useful for research scholars, students and faculty in Management, Adult Education, Sociology, Social Work and Human Resource Management. The book is a good resource book for worker educators, trade unionists and management experts.

Dr. Yerroju Bhaskaracharyulu

ACKNOWLEDGEMENTS

Ignorance is the root cause of all evils. The Hindu Upanishads preach ***Thama Soma Jyothirgamaya*** which means enlighten us from the darkness of ignorance. I am ever grateful to holy men for blessing me to concentrate on crises managements in the industrial field. Workers' Education is one of the important tools for crises management and accomplishment of a task of this nature is not my merit but the Divine Grace.

I take this opportunity to place on record my deep sense of gratitude to Prof. D.Subba Rao, former Director and Head of the Department of Adult and Continuing Education, Andhra University, Visakhapatnam, for providing me an opportunity to fulfil my ambition and for his valuable guidance throughout.

I am indebted to Dr. M.Gopalakrishna Reddy, former Vice-Chancellor, Andhra University, Visakhapatnam for his moral support in establishing myself in the present position. I am grateful to Prof. K.Jayashankar, former Vice-Chancellor, Kakatiya University, Warangal and Prof. Y.C.Simhadri, Vice-Chancellor, Andhra University, Visakhapatnam whose blessings and best wishes bestowed on me and enabled me to mould my career and complete this work.

My grateful thanks to my beloved friends Prof. K.Kameswara Rao, Dept. of Environmental Sciences and Dr. D.V.R.Murthy, Associate Professor, Dept. of Journalism and Mass Communication, Andhra University for their critical comments and helpful discussions.

I sincerely thank Prof. C.S.Venkata Ratnam, Director, GIFT, Visakhapatnam, for his valuable suggestions and encouragement.

It is my duty to duly acknowledge the officials of the CBWE for providing me access to the information.

The successful completion of this work would have not been possible but for the moral support given to me by my wife, Sandhya Nirmala and my daughters, Sarath Jyothsna and Swetha Madhavi, my son-in-law Chakrapani whose patience, encouragement and time sacrifice are invaluable.

My special thanks are due to my colleagues, friends and co-scholars for creating a congenial atmosphere throughout the course of my study.

—Dr.Yerroju Bhaskaracharyulu

LIST OF ABBREVIATIONS USED

AITUC	:	All India Trade Union Congress
APPM	:	Andhra Pradesh Paper Mills Ltd.
BC	:	Backward Castes
BHPV	:	Bharat Heavy Plate and Vessels Ltd.,
BMS	:	Bharatiya Mazdoor Sabha
CBWE	:	Central Board for Workers' Education
CFTU	:	Central Federation of Trade Unions
CITU	:	Centre of Indian Trade Unions
DLB	:	Dock Labour Board
FACOR	:	Ferro Alloys Corporation
HMS	:	Hind Mazdoor Sabha
ILC	:	International Labour Conference
ILO	:	International Labour Organisation
INTUC	:	Indian National Trade Union Congress
NEU	:	National Employees Union
NGO	:	Non Gazetted Officer
NJM	:	Nellimerla Jute Mills Ltd.
PSP	:	Praja Socialist Party
SC	:	Scheduled Castes
SLC	:	Standing Labour Committee
SRMT	:	Sri Ramadas Motor Transport Ltd.
SRMTU	:	Sri Ramadas Motor Transport Employees Union

ST	:	Scheduled Tribes
ULC	:	Unit Level Classes
UNESCO	:	The United Nations Educational Social and Cultural Organisation
UK	:	United Kingdom
USA	:	United States of America
USSR	:	Union of Soviet Socialist Republics
UTUC	:	United Trade Union Congress
VPT	:	Visakhapatnam Port Trust
WEP	:	Worker's Education Programme
WT	:	Worker Teachers

INTRODUCTION

Industrial development has been a major hope of finding solution to the 02/04 problems of poverty, insecurity and over population. Nehru said as "real progress must ultimately depend on industrialisation". Throughout the world, industrialisation has indeed become the magic word of the 20th century. The reasons for this explosion of interests in industrialisation is to raise the productivity of the labour force, increased national output and, thus, lead to a better income to the poor and underprivileged.

Thus, economic growth has become a major factor of world economic policy in the recent decades. Since World War II, there was a remarkable intensification of interest in economic growth both in the developed and developing countries for various reasons of economic, social and political. Apart from the individual countries, International Labour Organisation and the United Nations and its specialised agencies have addressed themselves to the task of promoting rapid economic growth. International Labour Organisation (ILO) is instrumental in promoting the cause of Workers' Education in a majority of the countries, and especially in the developing and the under developed world. The Indian Workers' Education Programme also has been guided by the ILO from time to time.

India, after independence, in order to develop its economy at a faster rate and to achieve self-reliance, increased its investments on the industrial sector. However, productivity was often clouded with the problems in industrial relations mainly due to the fact of illiterate and uneducated work force. Thus, the Government began to seriously plan Workers' Education during the later half of the 1950s and established the Central Board for Workers Education in 1958.

The Central Board for Workers' Education (C.B.W.E.) has designed several programmes, all aimed at developing an educated work force. One of the important programmes of the C.B.W.E. is training of workers by their colleagues who are trained as Worker Teachers. The trade unions will arrange to organise the programme for which the grants-in-aid will be provided by the C.B.W.E. while concerned managements are supposed to provide facilities.

The Scheme, on one hand is to create a sense of trade union consciousness among the workers and on the other, should enable the trade unions to do away with outside leadership by finding leadership from amongst the rank and file of members.

The programme, because of its vital importance needs unbiased evaluations and assessments from time to time, so as to review the approach and methods of the scheme to realise the desired objectives. Such assessments and evaluations have to be made by persons not directly involved in the Scheme. Some of the universities have taken interest in evaluating the Workers' Education Programme at National, Regional and Local levels. Kakkar[1], Rizvi Khan[2], Gandhi[3] and Sivapalan[4] have made critical evaluations of the programme aspects.

The present study investigated the impact of the Workers' Education Scheme in some selected Public and Private Sector undertakings at the C.B.W.E. region of Visakhapatnam, which covers Srikakulam, Vizianagaram and Visakhapatnam and East Godavari districts of Andhra Pradesh.

The present work is presented in three parts and seven chapters. The first part consisting of three chapters, provide background study with several facts and a detailed review.

Chapter I reviews Trade Unionism in India and the need for Workers' Education Programme in envisaging stronger trade unions and self reliant in leadership. The influence of ILO's Workers' Education activities on the Workers' Education Programme in India and abroad is described.

Chapter II delineates Workers' Education Scheme at the National, State and Local Region levels with a special emphasis on the organisation and implementation. A comparative analysis is made between the ILO activities and the Indian Programme.

Chapter III introduces the present study, its aims and objectives along with a brief discussion on similar studies in India and abroad.

The second part is presented in three Chapters. Chapter IV describes the methods and the approach adopted for the study. Different questionnaires have been developed and several interviews were conducted with various personnel of the Government, Central Board for Workers' Education, Departments of Industrial Relations and Personnel Management, Sociology, Adult and Continuing Education etc. The range of people covered extended from workers attending unit level classes to the authorities in the Central Board for Workers' Education.

Chapter V is the analysis of the data obtained and reflects the views of the participating workers, Worker Teachers, trade union leaders and managements with special reference to age, sex, experience, education and qualifications. Based on these, in Chapter VI, the impact of Workers' Education Scheme is discussed, along with a discussion on the relevance of, and acceptability of the scheme. The major findings of the study are briefly discussed with special reference to the objectives of the ILO and C.B.W.E. to fulfil the study objectives.

The final Chapter of third part provides a summary of the findings of the study and suggests prime area for further studies, which help in promoting the cause of Workers' Education at Visakhapatnam Region.

REFERENCES

1 Kakkar, N.K., *Workers' Education in India*, Sterling Publishers (Pvt.) Ltd., New Delhi, 1973.

2 Rizvi Khan, *Impact of Workers' Education Schemes on Industrial Relations: A Diagnostic Study*, UGC Project Report, Aligarh Muslim University, Aligarh, 1971.

3 Gandhi, Kalyani, *Workers' Education Scheme of India*. Doctoral Thesis, The State University of New Jersey, USA, 1979.

4 Sivapalan, T.R. Unnithan, *An Enquiry into the Workers' Education Programme in Kerala with a view to Suggest Improvements*. Doctoral Thesis, University of Kerala, Trivandrum, 1990

PART—I

1

TRADE UNIONISM AND WORKERS' EDUCATION

Trade unions are, perhaps the biggest mass organisations in most countries, whether those which have a developed market economy or those which are broadly included in the Third World. The spirit of organisation has gripped the minds of large sections of workers and employees engaged in different economic and administrative sectors. Trade unions, generally, reflect the nation's socio-economic, industrial and political life as a whole. They are generally understood as voluntary organisations of workers formed with different models of unionism,[1-4] for the purpose of defending and advancing the collective interests of the workers or employees either mutually or in relation to other parties such as employers, government and other trade unions.[5, 6]

The concept of Trade Unions, is the result of Industrial Relations. "Industrial Relations is that part of management which is concerned with the manpower of the enterprise[7]. Manpower of the enterprise can broadly be classified as management and workers, or employers and employees, and the Industrial Relations can be treated as the relations within the industry mainly between management and workers, where trade unions can play an important role. It is realised that the effectiveness of the management largely depends on how the manpower of the enterprise contributes its best towards the attainment of corporate objectives. Industrial Relations can play a number of functions. Some of the important functions of Industrial Relations are:

1. to establish a pipe line between the workers and management;
2. to establish a rapport between managers and management;
3. to ensure creative contributions of the Trade Unions;
4. to avoid industrial conflicts;
5. to safeguard the interests of both workers and management;
6. to bring about government control over the industry;
7. to raise the industrial productivity, and above all;
8. to establish and maintain the industrial democracy.

However, in India, the influence of these functions on many of the healthy factors is strikingly meagre. Sethi and Krishnan[8] observed that "the central values of our country's Industrial System appears to be competition, class struggle and compromise. Broadly, employers and their managers by and large consider Trade Unions and Trade Union leaders as "nuisance", or "hurdle", or at best "unavoidable nuisance" or "unavoidable hurdle"[9]. Hence, with a view to establish harmonious employer-employee relations, the labour management committee of the Asian Regional Conference of the ILO has laid down certain fundamental principles as 'objections of social policy in governing Industrial Relations'.

The history of the Industrial Relations in India can be classified into various periods, namely, pre-medieval period, ancient period, medieval period, British period and modern period. In ancient India, hunting, agriculture, handicrafts, barter economy etc., are some of the areas where systematic practice of human/industrial relations are observed. Varnashrams provide evidence for the existence of the concept of division of labour. During medieval period, Kautilya has created number of productive occupations. Various types of guild systems, namely, artisans' guild, merchants' guild and co-operative guild etc., though hampered organised Industrial Relations, the existence of Piga and Shreni Unions achieved good Industrial Relations[10].

Industrial Relations during the ancient period as well as during the period of Hindu rulers were quite cordial, which were based on mutual respect and understanding, and these foundations were shaken during the period of Muslim rulers on whose whims and fancies the Industrial Relations were maintained[11]. The situation continued till the British period.

The death of a European Railway contractor in 1859 forced the Central Government to pass the first Industrial Relations Act in 1860 (Employers' and Workmen's (Disputes) Act of 1860). However, the workers were not satisfied and they were actually in a very deplorable condition.

In order to draw the attention of Government to the wretched conditions of the workers and the need for legislation, an agitation was launched by Mr.Sorabjee Shapurjee Bengalee, in the year 1875. The trade unions movement in India said to have begun with this event.[12] Later, in the year 1890, under the leadership of Mr. N. M. Lokhande, the Bombay Millhands Association was formed which is known as the first labour Association in India.[13] A large number of labour associations were started in the country. But most of these were not viewed as trade unions in proper sense, as these organisations of workers were not like a continuous body, but they were merely ad-hoc committee formed for the purpose of specific grievances on specific occasions.[13] The movement gained momentum with the birth of Buckingham and Carnatic Mill Workers' Organisation in the year 1918, subsequent to which several organisations sprang up and led to the formation of All India Trade Union Congress in 1920 which was successful in forcing the government to pass the Trade Union Act, 1926.

Trade Unions in India can be classified into three types–Craft Unions, General Unions and Industrial Unions.[14] When the trade union is formed by the workers of the same occupation, irrespective of the distinction of the industry where they are working, such unions are called 'Craft Unions'. Andhra Pradesh Auto Driver's Union, Municipal Sanitary Workers' Union of Andhra Pradesh etc., are some of the examples. All workers in a single industry irrespective of the craft, grade or skill, when organised under one union is called an 'Industrial Union'. Electricity Workers' Union, Transport Employees' Union, Textile Workers' Union are some of the Industrial Unions. The 'General Union' stands as one mega union and admits any worker. Indian National Trade Union Congress (INTUC), Hind Mazdoor Sabha (HMS), Centre of Indian Trade Unions (CITU), All India Trade Union Congress (AITUC), United Trade Union Congress (UTUC) are the examples of General unions. Craft unions tend to become 'Occupational' catering for a number of related crafts, while the Industrial Unions are sometimes more directly 'Common Employment Unions' say, the employees of a single employer or recognisable group of employers and General Unions can admit anybody or affiliate any union.

Trade Unions are also often recognised as various other types such as Blue-collared unions (usually referred to unions of workers whose job is related to physical labour) and White collared unions (e.g. NGO unions; Clerical staff unions; Teachers' union etc.)[15, 16] Hoxle, classified trade unions based on their functional types. Five such types were recognised which differ in their group psychology: (a) business unionism; (b) friendly unionism; (c) revolutionary unionism; (d) predatory unionism and (e) dependent unionism.

Trade Union consciousness is very high among the Indian workers, especially in urban industrial workers than in rural ones. The rate of unionisation in older industries, such as textiles, jute, railways etc., have a greater degree of unionisation and as early in 1968, there were about 13,000 registered unions of workers with the membership of above 5 million. Roughly 60 per cent of the total unions are affiliated to one or the other national centres.[17] The four principal national centres – the AITUC, the INTUC, the HMS and the UTUC, are in turn known to have affiliations with different political parties.* The structure of unions is primarily organised at the enterprise level. The next stage constitutes their association or federation at the industry level. At the apex, they have affiliation with their respective national centres. Broadly, this is a 3-tier system whereas at enterprise level unions devote themselves to job-related questions, such as wages and benefits, other rules of work and problems of the work place. Those organised at the industry level provide a federating link to

* C.P.I (AITUC), Congress (I) (INTUC), P.S.P. Group (HMS) and Radicals I and II (UTUC).

enterprise unions. In addition, they attend to industry wise issues and participate in forums dealing with industrial problems. The national centres are involved in political and broad policy issues of interest to unions and workers. This division of tasks need not, however, be rigid. It may change from unit to unit, place to place and from time to time, of course, as demanded by time.

The fundamental aim of the Trade unions is to protect the interests of the workers. All the Trade unions in India will have at least three objectives in common. The first one is related to bring about a change in the economic status of the workers, the second one to overthrow capitalism and stimulate a change in the political order and the third one is to eliminate managerial dictatorship by workers' democracy and bring about a change in the social order.[18]

Although there is a greater overlap among the objectives of the Trade unions, several parallel unions have developed with deviations in the approach to realise their objectives and of course, problems of sharing the responsibility, political ideology etc., also form other important factors.

Strength, security and confidence are the three important returns, the members of the Trade unions would expect. Above all, the most important social purpose of the Trade unionism is, the participation in job regulation. But, participation is not an end in itself, it is the means of enabling workers to gain more control over their working lives.[19] A worker through his union will have more direct influence and participation in respect of framing rules and their implementation, than he can ever exercise by his vote to the State.

Lack of organisation results in weakness. Similarly, illplanned functioning erodes the strength of the organisation. Thus, proper leadership with positive guidance and strong trade unions with enlightened members are among the prime factors which enable successful functioning of the Trade Unions. However, in India, a vast mass of industrial labour is illiterate, a state of affairs which is unknown to any other country of industrial importance. The situation was still worse when the movement of Trade Unions were gaining momentum 60 years ago.[20] Owing to the economic crises during the post-independence period, the plight of the workers was so disastrous and created serious set backs in the industrial production, inflating the economy, and the growth of Trade Unions spread like a wildfire to safeguard the interests of the workers. In 20 years, the number of Trade Unions in India rose by 17 times while the membership in the trade unions has increased by 8 times till 1985 (Table 1.1).

Table—1.1

Growth dynamics of trade unions and their membership

			Growth		*Membership*
Year	*Total No.of Unions*	*Membership n × 1000*	*Unions (%)*	*Membership (%)*	*Mean No./Unions*
1920	107	141	–	–	132
1940	666	511	522	262	767
1961	11,416	3,960	1,614	675	347
1966	14,370	4,369	26	10	304
1971	22,121	5,431	54	24	246
1976	28,924	5,447	31	>1	188
1985	42,985	7,362	49	35	171
1991	52,773	6,094	23	171	115
1993	54,969	3,129	04	487	56
1994	24,912	4,093	-55	308	164
1995	32,811	6,516	32	592	198
1996	35,895	5,606	9	-140	156
1997	34,652	7,372	-3	315	213

Reoriented after: Indian Labour Statistics, 1977 & 1979; Pocket Book of Labour Statistics, 1981, P.C. Tripathi and C.B.Gupta, Industrial Relations and Labour Laws, Sultan Chand & Sons, New Delhi, 1990, p.65

Statistical Abstract, India 2000, Central Statistical Organisation, Ministry of Statistics & Implementation, Govt. of India, New Delhi, pp.312-313.

The peculiar situation of Trade unionism in India is that, it is influenced by a number of factors, such as political motivations through outside political leaders at the top of the Trade Unions; exploitation of unions by vested interests of individuals; multiplicity of the unions and intra-union rivalries; low level of trade union consciousness; meagre financial resources and above all a low level of workers' education. Membership of each union becomes insignificant when Trade Union consciousness is very low. Presence of multiunionism also influences the membership growth in each union and leads to unsound financial state. The membership of the unions depends on the political power of the parties to which the union is affiliated. The membership of the union will be greater, if the political party to which it is affiliated is greater in power. The political influence on the trade unionism is perhaps one of the most important handicaps of the trade unionism in India.

In India, Industrial Sector is becoming a Sector of increasing disputes. Number of strikes and lockouts and the workers involved in it are increasing significantly day-by-day. The industrial revolution in England, with the protective legislative measures/ the development of ILO at Geneva and the general support given to the working class by the National movement in India have contributed to labour legislative measures in India to a larger extent. The recommendations of the Royal Commission on Labour, 1931 and the Labour Investigation Committee, 1946 unearthed the deficiencies in the labour legislative measures and suggested suitable labour legislative activity. However, experts on the labour legislation opined that the labour legislation in India has not been able to cover certain categories of labour such as domestic labour, rural labour and of many in the unorganised sector.

Apart from the Labour Legislations, Social Security legislations were also developed. Social Security programmes and benefits in India have been in existence since times immemorial. But organised Social Security measures in statutory form are only of recent origin, that too for industrial workers only. Social Security Legislation in India is to protect the workers and consists of so many enactments.[21] All these Social Security measures and to protect the workers from the hazards of income insecurity, occupational insecurity and natural insecurity. Lord Beveridge defined Social Security as "an attack on five giants – want, disease, ignorance, squalor and idleness". The need for Social Security measures in India is highly essential, since 60% of the industrial units are under Private Sector. If poverty and unemployment are problems in Indian context, on the contrary the gauge of high industrialisation has created new problems in the advanced nations.

It is said that Social Security schemes at present, in force cover a small fraction of the total working population. Some degree of Social Security is no doubt provided for lakhs of industrial workers but millions of workers engaged in agriculture, smaller establishments, domestic works etc., are barely left without any protection. Besides, it is criticised that the Social Security legislations suffer from narrow scope, inadequacy of benefits, overlapping rules and with different administrative defects and impediments to enforcement. The study group of 1957-1958 appointed by the Government of India has recommended for integration of various Social Security measures with common goal of contribution.

If Labour Legislations encouraged strong Trade Unions, Social Security legislations wanted to drive the ignorance of the work force so as to equip themselves with security. Thus, Labour Education has assumed increasing importance as the vast masses of Indian labour are illiterates.

In spite of rapid growth in the number of trade unions, the membership growth in individual union has not maintained the pace, while multiunionism in individual sectors, to a considerable extent, weakened the unions, their finances and sometimes their very existence. Due to the political influence, the membership of the individual trade unions has been adversely affected especially in undertaking several common programmes. Very few trade unions have seriously taken the cause of Workers' Education. The awareness levels of workers have remained low and thereby their loyalty to the Trade unions remained to be regulated by the above described political influence and other factors.

The Government of India has also recognised that the absence of education among labour is the root-cause for many troubles– lack of good industrial relations, defective leadership, industrial unrest etc., and in pursuit to educate labour, Government has committed to various educational programmes in India. The content of Labour Education Programmes and activities have grown and developed in pace with the evolution of work, organisations, changing conditions of work, labour management relationships and most important of all, the acceptance of new concepts relating to the increasing rights and responsibilities of the organised labour in the social and economic life and development of nation, community and enterprise[23]. Central Board for Workers' Education, Indian Institute of Workers' Education, Educational wings of Trade Unions, Managements, Universities etc., are some of the agencies actively engaged in to cater the needs of the labour and aspirations of the Government.

Labour Education is specially designed to involve workers of different sectors, in educative programmes aimed at the development of skills, knowledge, understanding and to motivate them to participate in institutional, social, economic and enterprise development. "Education" as said by our Late Prime Minister, Smt.Indira Gandhi, is not merely the accumulation of information, but the discipline of mind that makes for balanced, well adjusted person who is capable of meeting the changing challenges of life.[24] The inspiring thoughts of Smt.Indira Gandhi provided a great deal of guidance for the various agencies involved in Labour Education Programmes. The Five Year Plan Draft Reports recognised the need for improving the quality of industrial labour, who were considered illiterate. Modern machine industry depends on a peculiar degree of education; and the attempt to build it up with an illiterate body of workers must be difficult and perilous. Thus, the education of industrial labour should be dealt with an increasing priority.

Table—1.2 shows the literacy rate of population and industrial labour in India. The literacy rate of industrial labour appears meagre when compared to population literacy rate during 1961-2001.

Workers' Education in India, incorporates diversed educational programmes, ranging from General Adult Education, Vocational Education, Population Education, Women Education and Rural Workers' Education etc. Adult Education is an intrinsic part of life long education. Vocational education is complimentary to professional and occupational education. Population Education is fundamental and integral part of the socio-economic development process and aims at to spread the implications of Population increase, to create an understanding that Family Welfare Planning does not only mean population control but also family and social welfare to stimulate the acceptance of the need for the small family norms of workers etc. Women's Education is a specialised curriculum meant for women introduced at various levels–University Departments, Colleges, Home Science Institutes, Polytechnics etc., to impart education to women in India. The Estimates Committee of Parliament in its Fourth Report, 1971-72 recommended to extend education to agriculture labour also. In concurrence to this, the Central Board for Workers' Education in its 56th Meeting held in 1976 at Mangalore decided to intensify its programmes for Rural Workers through Non-formal Education Programmes. Non-formal Education is a compliment to formal education and is free from constructive and restrictive influences of formal education. It meets the needs of learners of different categories at their door-steps.

Table—1.2

Growth of literacy rate of population and industrial labour

Year	*Total Population (in millions)*	*Literacy Rate (%)*	*Industrial Labour (in millions)*	*Industrial Labour (% of total Population)*	*Literacy Rate (% of Industrial Labour)*
1961	439.2	24.02	162.2	36.93	18.92
1971	548.2	29.46	203.4	37.10	20.14
1981	685.2	36.23	263.2	39.41	38.82
1991	843.9	52.21	314.1	37.50	NA
2001	866.8	65.38	NA	NA	NA

Re-oriented after:

Indian Labour Journal, 1982.

An analysis of situation of children in India, New Delhi, NICEF, 1984, pp. 15 & 63

Census of India, 1991

Census of India, 2001

Labour Bureau, Ministry of Labour, Govt. of India, New Delhi.

Workers' Education in particular deals with educational needs of workers to improve their individual and group competence and advancement to their social, economic and cultural interest. It helps the worker to become a responsible citizen and a duty minded union member. All the philosophers of the world, irrespective of the age, in which they lived, believed in work, productivity and the worker. The ancient varna system of Hindus, according to which the society is classified into four varnas based on their profession and skills. Then skill in the particular profession was considered to be the education they needed. The purpose of work was to hold the society together and to make on self reliant. Thus, the welfare of the workers is the fundamental base for the welfare of the society.

The advent of mechanisation of civilisation and rapid socio-economic changes that took place during the past two centuries have expanded the scope of Workers' Education in order to balance their position in the society. Incidentally, all the present developed countries have better programmes for their Workers' Education. A brief review of Workers' Education Programmes in different countries is presented which may help in examining the programme in India.

Workers' Education in the United Kingdom

According to the modern economists "the working day could not be lengthened anymore, wages could not be lowered anymore, the health of the working class could not be undermined anymore without (in many cases) leading to complete cessation of work".[25] During the beginning of the 19th century, the object of the Workers' Education was defined by Workers' Educational Association as "the promotion of the higher education of the working people, primarily by the extension of University Teaching",[26] and to achieve through:

(a) the assistance of working class efforts of a special educational character;

(b) the assistance in the development of an efficient school continuation; and

(c) the co-ordination of popular educational effort.

The Workers' Educational Association made alliance with universities and by 1908 its branches numbered 50 and promoted the university extension courses and rounded up audience for them. The service of Workers' Educational Association in the field of Adult Education is described as a movement by a common belief in the importance of education. The Workers' Educational Association is in the form of a federation, open to working class and educational bodies as well as to individual members.[27] The Workers' Educational Association's original purpose was "to stimulate and to satisfy the demands of its adults, in particular members of the workers' movements for education by the promotion of courses and other facilities and generally to further the advancement of education to the end that all children, adolescents and adults may have full opportunities for the education needed for their complete individual and social development.[28]

The subject areas of chief concern have been the social and economic studies that provide the background for voluntary action in social work, politics, trade unions and local governments, though there is also a very substantial provision for classes in literature, music, local studies and the arts and organising of the classes is carried out by voluntary local branches with the help of a small number of professional tutor organisers. The class is a self governing exercise in learning, the tutor and students working out their programme of study together and modifying in the light of their progress.

The Workers' Educational Association was recognised as a 'responsible body' in 1924. The growth of the extramural departments made most Universities in the U.K. depend on Workers' Educational Association for arranging classes. It is now holding link with almost half the number of courses run in the country. Workers' Educational Association being a 'non-party political and non-sectarian' association, has a unique stand in its activities and courses, and has developed great nexus between universities and industries to cater the needs of socially deprived communities.

The courses conducted by Workers' Educational Association are:

1. three-year courses of at least 24, an-hour meetings per year;
2. One year courses of at least 20, 1½-hour meetings;
3. Terminal courses of not less than 10, 1½-hour meetings;
4. Residential courses and training courses for teachers and lecturers in adult education;
5. Short-term summer courses of 6 meetings.

Courses requiring not more than 10 meetings are grouped as other courses.

Workers' Education in the United States of America

The Workers' Education as practiced in the United States primarily deals with the educational needs of workers and enables their active participation in the trade union movement. The American Workers' Education Programme aims at the general improvement of workers' individual and group competence, to make the worker 'mature, wise and responsible' citizen by advancing his social, economic and cultural interests. It enables him to play his part as a trade union member and also as a social being.

Various types of Workers' Educational programmes are there in the USA which cover a wide range of vocational, apprenticeship training, trade, adult education etc. While the motive of "Workers' Education" is trade union education, almost all trade unions in the USA have their own educational programmes and concept of Workers' Education in the USA changed with the growth of the trade union movement. Initially, the socialist ideas prevailed in Europe and Great Britain influenced the American trade union leadership in the early decades of the 19th century when general belief was to use education as a power to change the social order. The first school for workers, known as the Working Men's Institute was established at John Hopkin's University in 1879. Later, the socialist movement of American influenced the trade unions, institutions and intellectuals during the early 20th century. The campaign of the socialists through study circles, labour colleges, pamphlets and public speeches spread the aims of socialism and established the Rand School of Social Sciences.

The Ladies Garment Workers' Union established in 1914 was the first recognised institution of Workers' Education in the USA. Though the American Workers' Education was influenced by Europe, there were two main groups among them. The one aimed at a social change through the labour movements while the other, at the individual development of the worker. The participation of the universities was not accepted by the working class in its spirit because they, unlike those in European countries, looked at the universities with suspicion.

The Federal Government came to support Workers' Education by organising programmes under Federal Emergency Relief Administration and in first ten years about ten million workers were trained in these programmes. It marked the beginning of the involvement of state in the education programmes for workers. The objectives of Workers' Education were re-defined in terms of labour problems of particular concern to the workers.

Most of the Workers' Education Programmes were conducted directly by the trade unions, though certain universities run courses for workers, are based on the support of the trade unions. The use of increasing automation necessities training and re-training the worker and vocational education initiated by the concerned union. The trade unions as a whole are responsible for the education given to their members to bring about a more effective industrial relations, stronger unions and better standards of living in the USA.

Workers' Education in Germany

The German Workers' Education is exclusively related to the activities of the workers' organisations and are completely separated from the general adult education programmes in the country. An academy in Germany, "*Arbeit und Leben*" which means work and life, has tried to link Workers' Education with general education and launched a progrmme in which young workers were given basic general education in communication, social sciences, and techniques of thinking and studying. Its methods stress the inter-relationship of subject matter, comradely give and take behaviour between teachers and students.[29]

Though the universities in German Democratic Republic have little role in the Workers' Education, students have shown interest in the problems and practices of Workers' Education with the collaboration of *Arbeit und Leben* groups in studying the activities of Workers' Education. University level academics were established to conduct training for trade union leadership with the support of municipal and provincial funds.

Workers' Education in France

The Workers' Education Programmes are known in France from the late 19th century. The need was recognised by the trade unions and the local federation of trade unions were the initiators of Workers' Education Programmes. The three major trade unions in France, C.G.T., C.F.T.C. and F.O, organise classes on their own and the Government aid is sought and is given in varying degrees through various agencies.

The classes are organised periodically by different organisations and are tuned to the interests of the working class movements –"Schisms in these movements along political and religious lines have prevented the establishment of any kind of coordinating institution in labour education, as well any unified approach to the achievement of goals". Trade Unionism in France has close working relationship with UNESCO schools at *La Breviere*, Workers' Education Association's summer activities in Great Britain and co-operation from the American foreign aid agencies like E.C., M.S.A., F.O.A., and E.P.A.

The C.F.T.C. Workers' Education can be comparable to the American Workers' Education and employs many of the methods of American Workers' Education. French Universities show greater interest in Workers' Education. However, the Workers' Federations doubt whether these programmes would break the shackles of French academicians in subject and methodology and really touch the vital interest of the French worker. Even though the Government aid is given to them and the co-operation from the part of universities is extended, the federations of workers in France always keep themselves away from them in their attitudes.

Workers' Education in the Former USSR

The Soviet trade unions showed much interest in educating their members. The education given by them was based on the social set-up and was aimed at social development. Since, 1921, the first Trade Union School was established in Moscow, work was fundamental to the whole of the Soviet Education System from Creche onwards.[30] Labour training for school leavers was an important area. Soviet education was explicitly vocational. The reasons for this significance of vocational education in the former USSR were both ideological and economic.

The three facets of vocational education in the Soviet Union were:

1. Moral education in the desired attitude towards work
2. Training in practical works skills and habits and
3. Vocational guidance.

Educational bodies like 'Staknovite Schools' were the places where workers develop highly efficient method of work. These schools, together with lectures, seminars and clerical training offered by managements concerned also played a major role in the Workers' Education.

Workers' Education in the Peoples' Republic of China

China is one of the biggest countries in the world in size and in population. The Educational Policies are attuned themselves to its principles. In China, education is always linked with work. There are many workers' colleges run by factories, colleges run by farms, short-term courses run by Universities' Correspondence Courses and Vocational and Technical Schools to serve agriculture. There are 'travelling schools' and 'horse-back schools' which serve the purpose in villages. The concept of the Workers' Education in China is "the productive labour must exercise leadership in everything".

The task of educating workers in China was undertaken originally by trade unions, which started several schools for this purpose. These schools were later formed under China Labour College. The institutions engaged in Workers' Education are of three levels.

(a) *China Labour College:* The Chinese Labour College is intended for trade union leaders and other national level people;

(b) *Trade Union Cadre Schools:* Acting as institutions of higher learning: The trade union cadre schools provide training to the local trade unionists and the ordinary workers; and

(c) *Workers' Colleges:* Workers' College offers two-year courses in six fields related to labour education.

Workers' College being an important component of both the national higher education system and adult higher education, include spare time college which do not offer full time programmes. The main objectives of Workers' Colleges are:[31]

(a) to train the workers and enable them to take up professional and managerial posts in industry;

(b) to train, in rotation, in-service cadres and skilled personnel and

(c) to develop capacities of scientific research, consultancy and technical assistance to industry.

All Workers' Colleges have to be approved by and registered with the relevant educational authorities. By the end of 1985, the number of Workers' Colleges reached 863 with an enrolment of 2,60,211.

Workers' Colleges run by factories are called July 21 Colleges which exist both in the cities and the rural areas. They are based on a document issued on 21st July, 1968 by the then Chairman Mao. Hence, these colleges are called July 21 Colleges. A factory-run college differs from a regular university and is designed to train people in the factories in their actual production. Most of the teachers are experienced workers of the factory, but there are also engineers and other personnel who come from technical schools to teach on a part-time basis. The worker students of these colleges link the productivity of China with the country's needs.

Workers' Education in the Philippines

The programmes for Workers' Education have come into effect in the Philippines after the establishment of the "Workers' Education Centre" in 1954 with the collaboration of National Economic Council and the U.S.International Co-operation Administration. Initially, programmes were based only on the economic and social aspects of industries and industrial workers while in 1956, four institutions were started to train the officials of trade union education through a one-week training course in the beginning. The training team consisted of the instructors of the institute, school and college teachers, adult educators and other leaders of the society. The object of these training courses was that the participants must become Worker Teachers in the concerned trade unions and organise Workers' Education classes on their own.

The Labour Department of the country had helped to establish a centre, Residential Labour Training School in 1956, meant for conducting six-months intensive training courses for trade union leadership. The centre also organised a good library for the workers as well as for the public. The library contains visual aids also. The centre extended its regional centres to Manila, Bacolod and Devao from where resources were supplied to the regional workers and institutions. Workers' Education in Philippines works for the ideological orientation and moral reformation of its members.

Workers' Education in Japan

Perhaps Japan had been the first Asian country that started and organised Workers' Education. A Workers' training institute called *Rodo Koshujo* was started in 1915 and later there was a rapid growth in the programmes of Workers' Education because of the initiative shown by trade unions as well as political parties. Several schools were established in different parts of the country under the initiative of 'General Council of Trade Unions of Japan' and Japan's Federation of Trade Unions and a large number of courses were run by the schools and many publications came out to benefit the ordinary workers of the country.

The Japan Institute of Labour founded in 1958 had contributed much to the development of Workers' Education in Japan. It acted as a master trainer in Workers' Education and gave financial and other helps to the Workers' Education Programme in the country. The International Development Department of Japanese Confederation (DOMEI) also has programmes for developing the skills of the workers. Collective bargaining is the most common tool adopted in Japan to determine the conditions of the working class.[32]

Workers' Education in Sri Lanka

The Workers' Education activities in Sri Lanka were started by the Labour Department in 1960. Though the trade union system in Sri Lanka is pluralistic as in India, it is different from that in Singapore, Malaysia, Indonesia and Philippines. It even differs from that of India's at least in two aspects – (i) relatively a lesser need to direct Workers' Education as Sri Lanka is in line with the developed countries in respect of literacy with a rate of approximately 80%; and (ii) has its own unique experiments for an Asian country in its programme for higher education for workers.[33]

The Department of Labour, the Sri Lanka Foundation Institution (SLFI) and The Workers' Education Institute are the main institutes in the Workers' Education. Trade Unions have different political opinions, and so organiser separate courses of their own, but where the programmes are of similar interest they join together to support SLFI and Labour Departments.

The Workers' Education courses of the University Workers' Education Institute offer opportunity for the necessary skills. The main defect in the Workers' Education Programme in Sri Lanka is that it neglects the women workers account for almost 25% of the proletariate there. The types of sponsors for courses being run in Sri Lanka are:

1. those conducted by the trade unions having Marxist leaders;
2. those conducted by non-Marxist political parties; and
3. those which are not run by political parties or their unions.

The training programmes have two components. In addition to the trade union education, they give population education also. The University Workers' Education Institute offers free higher education to workers conforming to the University standard. The Institute started in 1970 as the Workers' Continuing Education Institute, was placed under the University. In 1975, a similar Institute, the Workers' Education Institute, was started, which offers a four year Degree/Diploma (evening course).

International Labour Organisation and Workers' Education

The decision making in India on the promotion of Workers' Education Scheme, has been greatly influenced by the ILO. During the same period when various committees and conferences were evolving and planning the Workers' Education Programme in India, the ILO has emphasised the growing importance of Workers' Education, especially in the industrially less advanced countries where trade unions are young and inexperienced, and has launched a massive programme for Workers' Education in the year, 1956. This has stimulated the process of launching Workers' Education Programme in India. Most of the ILO concepts have formed general base for the Workers' Education Programme. Thus a brief review of the objectives and programmes of Workers' Education of the ILO will help in understanding the Workers' Education Programme in India.

ILO has launched its Workers' Education Programme with an aim "to help equip the workers with the knowledge and understanding they need not only to carry out their functional and civic responsibilities in modern society but also to contribute fully to the whole process of economic growth and social development[34] The emphasis is that on meeting the new educational requirements of the workers that changes this need with the changing times.[35]

Among various views on the goals of Workers' Education expressed by different ILO specialists, the prominently common view was "Providing trade union leaders and representatives at various levels not only with the necessary skills, but also with the intellectual tools that will enable them to analyse the process in a critical way and to take measures in terms of proposals, negotiations and action, as appropriate", and Bent and Pihl defined Workers' Education as education for workers for the purposes of better enabling them:

— to run their own organisations in an effective and democratic way as active members, organisers, educators or officers at different levels and covering all the various activities needed for the immediate objective achievement and strengthening of the union (trade union training);

— to directly improve their standard of living and quality of life through general adult education and vocational training.

The ILO has clearly defined its role and co-operation in extending its services as can be seen from Article 10.1 of its constitution, which stipulates: "The functions of ILO shall include the collection and distribution of information on all subjects relating to labour, particularly the examination of several subjects"[36]

The major activities of the ILO include a variety of programmes as shown below:

The ILO helps trade union organisations to provide training and knowledge to their members with a view to enabling them to fulfil their trade unions' social and economic responsibilities.

By making technical contribution (provision of instructors, supply of publications) for training courses and educational meetings and awarding study grants to participants in seminars convened by international trade union organisations.

By sending experts on missions at the request of the public authorities and the trade union organisations of the countries concerned. The ILO extends its help to the trade union organisations to develop their own Workers' Education services.

By organising seminars and study sessions for persons with responsibilities in the field of Labour Education to study problems of interest in them.

By publishing Workers' Education manuals, simplified versions of these manuals, monographs and studies on regional and technical aspects of Labour Education.

By lending films and film strips of Workers' Education on labour questions.

By granting fellowships for advanced study abroad by persons with Workers' Education responsibilities in trade unions to enable them to undertake further study of Workers' Education techniques and subjects.

A detailed explanation of the Workers' Education Programme in India is explained in Chapter II.

REFERENCES

1. A Lozovsky, *Marx and the Trade Unions*, International Publishers, New York, 1942, p.20.
2. Clark, Kerr and others, *Industrialisation and Industrial Man; the Problems of Labour and Management and Economic Growth*, Harward University Press, Massachusetts, 1960.

3. Paul Fisher, *Union in Less Developed Countries: a Reappraisal of the Economic Role"*, North Western University Press, 1963.

4. Everett, M. Kassalow, *Unions New and Developing Countries*, North Western University Press, 1963.

5. Dr. Tyagi, B.P. *Labour Economics and Social Welfare*, Jai Prakash Nath & Co., Meerut, 1980, p. 106.

6. Same as (1) above.

7. L.L.Bethel, F.J., Atawater, G.H.E. Smith and H.H.Stackman, *Industrial Organisation and Management"*, 1977, p. 385.

8. C.Sethi Krishnan, *Workers' Participation and Industrial Relations in India, some Reflections*, Decision, Vol.5, No.3, July, 1978, p. 187.

9. *Ibid*.

10. P. Ghosh and Santhosh Nath, *Labour Relations in India*, Sultan Chand & Co., New Delhi, 1973, p. 5.

11. Michael, V.P., *Industrial Relations in India and Workers Involvement*, Himalaya Publishing House, Bombay, 1979, p. 9.

12. Dr.Tyagi, B.P., *Labour Economics and Social Welfare*, Jai Prakash Nath & Co., Meerut, 1980, p. 79.

13. Dr. Bhagoliwal, T.N., *Econcmic of Labour and Industrial Relations*, Sahitya Bhavan, Agra, 1982, p. 230.

14. Michael, V.P., *Industrial Relations in India and Workers' Involvement in Management"*, Himalaya Publishing House, Bombay, 1979, p. 90.

15. Pramod Verma and Surya Mukherjee, *Trade Unions in India*, Oxford & IBH Publishing Co., New Delhi, 1982, p. 91.

16. Hoxie Rober F., *Trade Unionism in USA*, 1923.

17. Punekar, S.D. and others, *Labour Welfare, Trade Unionism and Industrial Relations*, Himalaya Publishing House, Bombay, 1981.

18. Tripathi, P.C. and C.B.Gupta, *Industrial Relations and Labour Laws*, Sultan Chand & Sons, New Delhi, 1990, p. 55.

19. Nitish, R. De, *Economic Times*, 25-8-1977.

20. Report of Royal Commission on Labour, 1931, p. 27.

21. Workmen's Compensation Act, 1923

    The Employees State Insurance Act, 1948

    The Coal Mines Provident Fund and Miscellaneous Provisions Act, 1948.

    The Employees Provident Fund and Miscellaneous Act, 1952

    The Maternity Benefit Act, 1961.

    Payment of Gratuity Act, 1972, etc.

22. Giri, V.V. *Labour Problems in Indian Industry*, Asia Publishing House, Bombay, 1972, pp. 269-296.

23. John, R.W., Whitehouse, New Dimensions of Workers' Education, *Workers' Education*, CBWE, December, 1977, p. 18.

24. Role of Education and Development, *Workers' Education*, CBWE, October, 1982.

25. William Z. Foster, *Outline History of the World Trade Union Movement*, International Publishers, New York, 1956, pp. 31 & 32.

26. Pillai, K.S. *Non-formal Education*: A critical study of its function in the U.K., with a view to suggesting practical steps to be undertaken in India and particularly in Kerala, 1984, p. 137.

27. G.D.H. Cole, *Organised Labour*, George Allen and Unwin Ltd., and The Labour Publishing Co., Ltd., 1924, pp. 112-113.

28. Russel Committee Report : *Adult Education*–A plan for development, AMSU, London, 1973, p. 37.

29. Allice H.Cook and Agnes M. Doubts, *Labour Education Outside the Union*, New York School of Industrial and Labour Relations, Cornell University, New York, 1958, p. 52.

30. Thomas, J.J. *Soviet Education in the 1980s*. St. Martin Press, New York, 1983, p. 106.

31. Yu Bo and Xu Hong Yan, *Adult Higher Education*–A Case Study on the Workers' Colleges in the Peoples Republic of China, IIEP, UNESCO, Paris, 1988, p. 33.

32. Kuhatasan, K., Tennets of Industrial Society in Japan, *Workers' Education*, CBWE, Nagpur, January, 1975, p. 34.

33. Wesumperuma, D., Workers' Education in Sri Lanka, *Workers' Education*, CBWE, Nagpur, March, 1983, p. 37.

34. *The ILO in a Changing World*, Report of the Director General, ILC, 1958, ILO, Geneva, p. 31.

35. *Labour Education*, ILO, Geneva, 1989/2, p. 1.

36 Bent Pihl, *Role of Making Trade Unions Effective Agent for Change, Labour Education*, 1988/1, pp.6 and 7.

2

WORKERS' EDUCATION SCHEME IN INDIA

The principle of 'Shrama Eva Jayathe' sloganed by our late Prime Minister, Smt. Indira Gandhi, is the essence of the Indian ancient philosophies which have always had glorified work as Karmayoga or Kriyayoga and taught to seek our destiny by achievement of excellence in respective spheres of activity. Unfortunately, the ethics of work is on decline in the recent periods.

Most of the industrial unrests have their origin in the illiteracy, ignorance and innocence of the workers, who are being carried away by the notions of few people, who in most cases, are with vested interests. Rights and duties are correlative as the health of the industry and health of the work force. The concept developed by the Indian workers –give or go, do or die–in respect of a good number of agitations against industrial units must be changed through a process of planned educational curriculum, suitable to workers in India. The Indian Government has taken good initiation by opening new vistas of agencies to educate Indian workers, the Workers' Education Programmes.

The term Workers' Education has been described variously in different countries and by different persons, influenced by historical, sociological, economic and political factors.

Florence Peterson observes that Workers' Education is a special kind of Adult Education designed to give workers a better understanding of their status, problems, rights and responsibilities as workers, as union members, as consumers and as citizens.[1]

Sri G. Ramanujam, a veteran prominent Trade Union leader, who championed the cause of Workers' Education in India felt that workers should be educated on "Nation First Approach." According to him, Workers' Education should aim to make the worker a responsible citizen, a dedicated worker, a dutiful head of the family and a constructive Trade Union worker.[2]

Late Sri T.Anjaiah, the then Minister of State for Labour, Government of India, opined that Workers' Education should aim 'to strengthen among all sections of working class including rural workers, a sense of patriotism, national integrity, unity, amity, communal harmony, secularism and pride in being an Indian"– which gives a positive and new deal to Workers' Education in India.[3]

The Royal Commission on Labour,[4] Five Year Plans[5] and the other working groups of Labour Education almost unanimously felt the imperative need to improve the quality of working force in India through Workers' Education Scheme.

The need for some organised and sustained effort in the direction of equipping the workers to manage their union affairs, without external interference in their long term interests and those of the nation as a whole and of imparting them the necessary background knowledge of country's economic and social imperatives and the dynamic development in those areas, was recognised. But, the questions remained were: How to proceed in the matter? What kind of organisation should be set up? How and by whom it should be managed? And who should finance it?

To look into the above matters in consultation with the interests concerned, namely, workers, employers and other prominent social and education leaders, an eight member team was constituted by the government (the team included four foreigners, two from the USA, one from the UK, and one from Sweden – all trade union leaders actively engaged in Workers' Education activities in their own countries and four Indians). The team visited important industrial centres and had discussion with union leaders employers etc., on the various aspects involved in implementing the Workers' Education Programmes. In certain sectors, the trade unions voiced their reservation about the advisability of the government playing a positive role in promoting Workers' Education. However, while drafting the teams' report, the team unanimously emphasized that in India, the choice was either Government sponsored Nationwide Workers' Education Schemes or no scheme at all.

Based on the recommendations of the team and realising the fact that the country could not afford to wait for the normal process of general education to reach the working class and bring about gradual improvement, the Indian Government, undertook a programme entitled "Workers' Education Scheme" in the year 1958.

The purpose of the scheme was not merely to eradicate the illiteracy but to teach workers on the purposes, functions and administration of trade unions and to identify the importance of their role in contributing to the economy of the nation. With this goal in mind, the Central Board of Workers' Education was formed which developed a three stage programme. The first stage, consisted of four months training of education officers, who would train workers to become Worker Teachers in the second stage. The Worker Teachers during the third stage return to their work places and train their worker colleagues. The idea of training a few and they in turn training few more was adopted so as to achieve the desired mass effect in the shortest possible time, by means of infectious spread.

Aims and Objectives of the Workers' Education Scheme

The aims and objectives of the Workers' Education Scheme as recommended by the Workers' Education Review Committee and accepted by the Government of India are:

1. To strengthen among all sections of working class, including rural workers, a sense of Patriotism, National Integrity, Unity, Amity, Communal Harmony, Secularism and Pride in being an Indian;
2. To equip all sections of workers, including rural workers for their intelligent participation in social and economic development of the Nation in accordance with its declared objectives;

3. To develop among workers a greater understanding of the problems of their social and economic environment, their responsibility towards family members; and their rights and obligations as citizens; as workers in the industry, as members and officials of their trade union;
4. To develop leadership from among the rank and file workers themselves;
5. To develop strong, united and more responsible trade unions through more enlightened members and better trained officials;
6. To strengthen democratic processes and traditions in the trade union movement and
7. To enable trade unions themselves to take over ultimately the functions of Workers' Education.

These objectives, mostly concur with those of ILO's objectives. The first objective is an essential component for a country like India, where in the recent times racialism, regionalism, religion are growing at alarming levels. The second and third objectives envisage the workers to play their role effectively with socio-economic participation at macro and micro levels, and enable the workers to carry out their functional and civic responsibilities. The fourth, fifth and sixth objectives help in to develop strong trade unions with enlightened membership led by a genuine leadership from workers themselves thereby avoiding the leadership of outsiders. The seventh objective is to enable the trade unions to carry out programme on their own. Thus, the objectives of the Indian Workers' Education Programme, also can be said to have objectives more or less similar to those adopted by ILO.

The Central Board for Workers' Education is the product of a deliberate tripartite decision arrived at the Indian Labour Conference held on 11th and 12th July, 1957. The workers' group has the largest representation in the Board with 8 members, while the employers from the Public Sector and Private Sector are 5. The University Grants Commission and the Indian Adult Education Association are also have their representatives. The Central Government has three seats while four nominees of State

Government are nominated by rotation. There is also provision to co-opt three members. The Board annually elects a governing body consisting of five members representing labour, three employers and three representatives of Central Government and one from a State Government and one from the University Grants Commission. With the exception of C.I.T.U., other major Central Trade Union Organisations i.e., the I.N.T.U.C., A.I.T.U.C., H.M.S. and the B.M.S., are represented on the Board as well as in its Regional Advisory Committees. The Head Quarters of the Board is located at Nagpur and the organisation is spread in 49 Regional Centres under the Four Zonal Directorates (Appendix I). Figure 2.1 illustrates the organisation set-up of Central Board for Workers' Education.

The main objectives of the Board are:

1. to administer and implement Workers' Education Programme in the country to develop strong and more effective trade unions through better trained officials and more enlightened members;
2. to develop leadership from the rank and file and promote the growth of the democratic process and tradition in trade union organisation and administration and
3. to promote among workers a greater understanding of the problems of the economic environment and their privileges and obligations as union members, officials and family members and as citizens.

The Workers' Education Scheme framed by the team of experts from time to time is implemented by the Central Board for Workers' Education to educate labour working in different sectors in India. The Scheme possesses three stage system.

In the first stage of the scheme, qualified persons, (Master's Degree in Economics, Industrial Relations, Social Work, Adult Education, Commerce, or Education and three years experience of work in the labour field) will be recruited as Education Officers and they will be given four month's full time training by the Board. Nominees of trade unions are also admitted to the Education Officer's course to enable them to undertake Workers' Education Programme under the guidance of their unions.

Fig. 2.1 Organisational Set-up

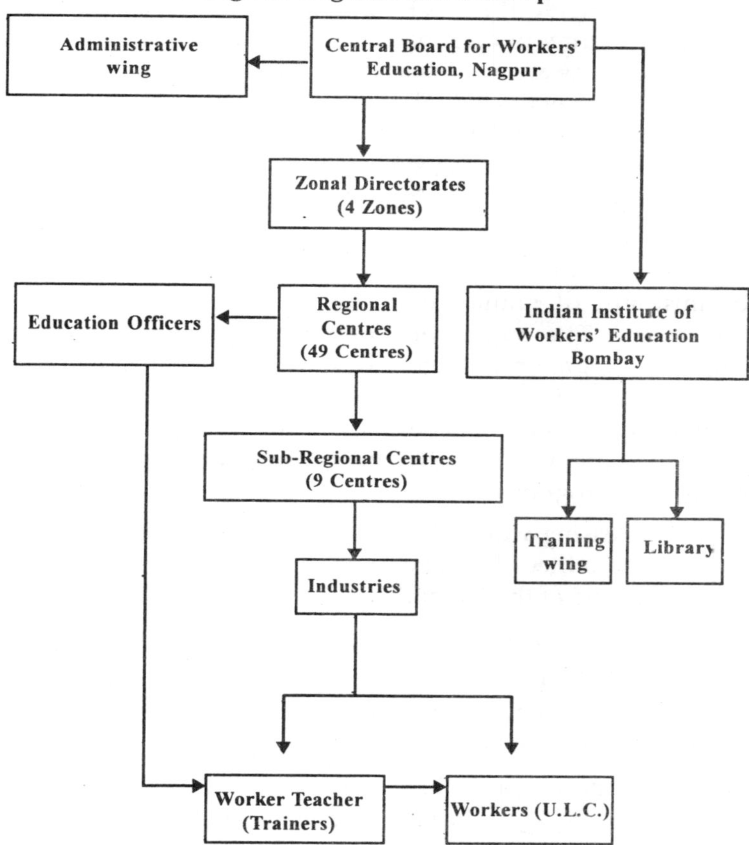

In the second stage, selected workers (The selection of worker teacher trainees is made by the Regional Advisory Committee of the Regional Centre. Trainees are sponsored by the trade unions and released by the employers with full wages for the training period) are trained at Regional and Sub-regional centres by the Education Officers. The workers thus trained, are called Worker Teachers (Trainers). They will be given full time continuous training of three months' duration in batches of 25-30.

During the third stage of Workers' Education Scheme, worker/teachers after completing their training come back to their places of work and conduct programmes for the rank and file of workers in Unit Level Classes. The Unit Level Classes are conducted outside the working hours. These classes will be conducted for three months, one hour a day for five days in a week, or if the facilities are available, three weeks full-time Unit Level Classes also be conducted. The syllabi of the Education Officers, Worker Teachers and Workers mainly emphasize topics related to trade unions, union-management relations, economics for trade unionists, labour legislation and workers' education (Appendices II-IV).

The vital link in the success of the programmes is the commitment of management to the Workers' Education Programme. The employers' participation in the Workers' Education Programme is reinforced by the recommendations of the Indian Labour Conference. Convinced that the educated and enlightened worker would be an asset to the industry and would also help to promote collective bargaining, employers agreed to support this programme by:

- *(a)* releasing workers sponsored by the trade union/local committees for being trained as Worker Teachers for a period of three months;
- *(b)* paying wages to worker teacher trainees for three months training period;
- *(c)* providing time-off for 45 minutes to enable the workers to attend the Unit Level Classes, and
- *(d)* supporting as far as possible, three weeks full-time Unit Level Classes instead of one and half hours per day, classes for three months.

In addition to these, the employers are giving voluntary contribution to the Worker Teachers during their study tour. The employers' representatives on the Central Board for Workers' Education and Regional Committees have been playing an active role.

Manuel Dia, an expert of the ILO for the Asian region, suggested a syllabi that can be relevant to courses on the same subjects in other countries. The Programme consists of three types of courses: Basic, specialised and advanced courses. The first set of training course suggested, leads to the next set and so on.

Conversely, the specialised and advanced courses build on the initial exposure and preparation of the basic courses.[7] The flow chart of course progamme is as follows:

Basic courses

- Basic trade union course
- Basic labour leadership course

Specialised courses

- Collective bargaining course
- Shop steward course
- Trade union administration course
- Occupational safety and health officer's course of trade unions
- Trade union research and information course
- Social welfare legislation course
- Trade union educators' course
- Co-operatives in the service of trade unions
- Labour dispute settlement
- Trade unions and productivity
- Training for works council representatives
- Development of appropriate training technology for Workers' Education

Advanced courses

- Executive development course for trade unions
- Project feasibility studies for socio-economic project for Trade Unions
- Trade unions and the national development
- Workers' participation in decision making
- Trade union advocates courses
- Labour policy studies
- Co-operative management course
- Job evaluation and wage and salary administration

Compared to this syllabi suggested by Manuel Dia[7], the syllabi for Worker Teachers appears to have a greater overlap in the contents and components, but differ in the organisation of the programme.

The syllabi of the Indian programmes consists of 12 major components having varying emphasis. Each component consists of several topics. The order of the arrangements is debatable. The component on Productivity will be dealt without giving a base for economics. Collective Bargaining, co-operatives and similar vital aspects have not been given COMPONENT status and will appear scatterdly spread over in different components. Thus, it appears to have a lapse in the continuity, thereby including unnecessary confusion, to the learners whose basic education level is relatively very low.

However, the coverage is so wide, it encompasses nearly 60 heads under 12 components. Of these, the 12th component deals exclusively with teaching methods and skills, for which more than 1/3rd of the course period will be devoted. On the other hand, the syllabi for Worker learners (ULC), whose education level is still lower, covers more than 50 heads under 9 components to be taught in 60 hours in a period of 12 weeks. The main course content is more or less similar with that of Worker Teachers .

Another drawback in the structure of the course is, little scope is left to deal with the type of technical education that is needed by the workers which varies with the type of industry. Workers of all types of industries will have to study the same syllabi. Similarly, due consideration is not given to the level of education of the Worker learners while formulating the syllabi or planning the programme. A worker with primary school education and another with Pre-University education will attend to the same class and receive the same type of instruction. This is important especially in a country like India where a large mass of workforce are illiterates.

So far, 789 Education Officers were trained by the Board to educate Worker Teachers in Public and Private Sector undertakings (Table 2.1). the first Worker Teachers ' training course was started on 16th February, 1959 at Indore and 88,273 Worker Teachers are trained by 49 Regional Centres headed by Regional Directors during the Plan Periods (Table 2.1). The first Unit Level Class was conducted on 1st July, 1959 and 40,60,902 workers were trained in Unit Level Classes during the plan periods (Table 2.1).

Table—2.1

Number of Education Officers, Worker Teachers (Trainers), and Workers trained (U.L.C.) during plan periods (1958-2003)

Plan period	*Education Officers*	*Worker Teachers (Trainers)*	*Workers trained in ULC*
Second Plan (1958-61)	100	1,070	9,070
Third Plan (1961-66)	217	6,340	3,09,470
Annual Plans (1966-69)	59	9,055	4,19,823
Fourth Plan (1969-74)	36	14,856	8,02,394
Fifth Plan (1978-79)	44	15,166	7,20,458
Annual Plans (1978-79)	46	3,955	2,13,677
(1979-80)	–	3,927	1,35,891
Sixth Plan (1980-85)	56	15,984	6,67,160
Seventh Plan (1985-90)	78	6,588	2,79,114
Annual Plans (1990-91)	–	1,209	52,385
(1991-92)	24	1,305	52,424
Eight Plan (1992-97)	75	5,721	2,30,281
Ninth Plan (1997-2002)	–	2,737	1,12,171
Annual Plans (1997-98)	–	1,038	38,492
(1998-99)	–	566	31,147
(1999-2000)	–	443	21,983
(2000-2001)	–	203	10,996
(2001-2002)	–	500	7,262
(2002-2003)	54	467	5,206
Tenth Plan (2002-2007)	54	360	6,504
Total	**789**	**88,273**	**40,60,902**

Reoriented after 44th Annual Report & Accounts, 2002-2003, CBWE, Nagpur, p.99.

Worker Teachers will be paid an honorarium of Rs.70/- p.m. The managements will provide necessary accommodation, furniture, lighting etc., and time-off facility to the workers for attending the Unit Level Classes.

The Board developed special short term trade union programmes for members of works committees and joint management councils, trade union officials and white collared workers. One-day schools, three day seminars and study circles, refresher courses for Worker Teachers and worker trainees are also organised. With a view to meet the needs of trade union officials, the Board also started correspondence course on trade union organisation and administration. The duration of this course is six months. The Board has also conducted specialised courses on population education, participative education and trade union education at different levels.

The Board has also extended its educational programmes to rural workers. In addition to this, the Board has initiated adult education programmes to cater to the needs of the illiterate workers in traditional industries, plantations, mines and rural areas.

One of the objectives of the Central Board for Workers' Education is to train workers for leadership so that trade unions in the country are run by the workers themselves. Therefore, leadership development programmes were envisaged. The candidates chosen for this purpose would be from among the trained Worker Teachers , who have an aptitude for leadership and also from the outside sources of educated workers. In future, this leadership development programme will be assuming greater importance in the organised sector, while there will be a need for training courses in the unorganised and rural sectors and in many special categories.

The Grants-in-aid Scheme of the Board assists trade unions and educational institutions in developing their own Workers' Education Programmes. The scheme was introduced in the year 1960 and has developed considerably since then. It was modified and improved from time to time, after taking into consideration suggestions from trade unions. The rules and procedures have been simplified to meet the trade union needs. The Board encourages unions to undertake the Workers' Education Programmes by providing grants for operational expenses. This facility can be utilised by all trade unions registered and of having at least 3 years standing, whose membership has no restriction of race, caste, sex or religion. Since 1970, the amount dispersed to the 1,304 trade unions was Rs.1,75,55,949-62 till 31-3-2003 and the workers trained during this period were 6,24,349 (Appendix V).

The Regional Directors/Education Officers of the Board inspect the programmes and provide necessary guidance to the grantees in organising grants-in-aid programmes. The programmes conducted by the grantees should conform with the syllabus prescribed by the Board.

Popular methods of teaching and training are practised in Workers' Education Programmes in India at all levels. Discussions, Seminars, Debates, Role Plays, Symposia, Case Studies and other two way communication methods constitute some of the principal methods. Educational visits are also arranged for trainees to union offices, factories and multipurpose plan projects.

The Board has published for use in the regional centres, and Unit Level Classes – posters, film strips, flip charts, pictorial charts and graphs, flannel graphs, stickers, flash cards and films. Requirements of suitable literature and study material for workers in the language known to them have met by publishing textural booklets in 14 languages, in simple and lucid style. Textural and pictorial booklets have been brought out, 1117 printed and 768 revised/reprinted ones, so far. These have been published in Hindi, Malayalam, Kannada, Tamil, Telugu, Bengali, Marathi, Gujarati, Nepali, Punjabi, Assamese, Oriya, Urdu and English. The booklets are made available to the workers at a nominal price of 50 paise per copy. They are revised and brought up-to-date from time to time.

The Board publishes a quarterly journal, 'Workers' Education', which aims at updating the information of its Officers, Worker Teachers about various labour issues. In addition, each Regional Centre brings out monthly bulletin in the regional language with a view to supply the latest information to the Worker Teachers on the current topics and keep them in pace with the new developments on the labour front.

The Board has a separate institution called, Indian Institute of Workers' Education which is a well equipped institution with competent faculty. It gives demonstration and information service and acts as a nucleus around which specialised schemes for training and education to labour are evolved. It also serves as a clearing house of knowledge for regional and sub-regional centres of the Board. It conducts research in developing and perfecting methods and tools of teaching. The institute conducts national level programmes for the Board. Training for officers and for trade union leaders sponsored by central organisations and federations. It offers the subjects like trade union leadership development, trade union organisation and administration, changing role of trade unions, industrial relations, women trade unionists and their role in social and economic spheres, problems and status of working women, grievance procedure, labour legislation, productivity and national development, workers' participation in industry, wages, co-operatives and economic development, techniques of communication in family welfare and population education. It also offers specialised industrywise courses for trade unionists in banking, petroleum and chemicals, printing, electricity, co-operatives, cement, port and docks, transport and other industries.

Other organisations which provides vital support to the Workers' Education Programme includes ILO and various institutes. Since the beginning of the 1960s, the ILO's Workers' Education Programme has been actually involved in various kinds of fruitful collaborations with Central Board for Workers' Education. Many of the staff members of the Board have travelled abroad under the ILO Fellowship training programmes to study Workers' Education Institutions and Programmes in Europe and elsewhere. Subsequently, many of its senior officials have served as ILO experts in different countries. The ILO also brings fellows from other countries to India to learn about Workers' Education Programme conducted by the Central Board for Workers' Education. This amply shows that the ILO-CBWE relations have been genuine.

The major lacunae in the programme is that it is not having a proper feed back facility to review the progress. Most of the industries have no definite information, in connection with the trained personnel in their employees. Another major lacunae is lack of proper emphasis on the ILO component.

In spite of the role played by the ILO, and its activities of diverse range for the benefit of workers, the ILO is not given a due status. The subject related to ILO is to be taught in two hours/ units.

Broadly in the Indian context, Workers' Education provides the educational needs of the worker, as an individual for his personal evolution, as an operative for his efficiency and advancement, as a citizen for a happy and integrated life in the community, as a member of trade union for the protection of his interests and as a member of the working class. Workers' Education also helps to fill in the lacuna caused by illiteracy to create better understanding of workers and their role in the national economy, to prepare workers for effective collaboration with the management, to make them better citizens, to create leadership among the ranks of labour to replace outsiders in trade unions and ultimately to make them conscious of their rights and responsibilities.

There are at present a number of institutions, either wholly or partly sponsored by the Government of India which are also trying to educate the workers and trade union leaders. At present, in addition to the Central Board for Workers' Education, the National Labour Institute and the Central Labour Institute with the Regional counterparts in Kolkata, Kanpur and Chennai (all these come under the Labour Ministry); Indian Adult Education Association; Workers' Social Education Institutes; Shramik Vidyapeeths, (now Janasikshana Samsthans) Universities and Labour Welfare Institutes are dealing with one or the other aspects of Workers' Education. In addition to these institutions, the Administrative Staff College of India (Hyderabad) and Institutes of Managements (Bangalore, Ahmedabad and Kolkata) are also organising Workers' Education Programmes. The activities of all these institutes can be co-ordinated through a network of Regional Centres to get the benefit at a faster rate. The CBWE has a good network of Regional Centres, through which it reached almost all corners of the Country.

The Central Board for Workers' Education has established 10 Regional Centres during 1959. The first regional centre was opened at Indore in February, 1959 followed by other Regional Centres at Hyderabad, Delhi, Dhanbad, Calcutta, Bombay, Bangalore, Kanpur, Alwaye and Nagpur in quick succession and now 49 Regional Centres and 9 Sub-Regional centres are functioning in our Country (Appendix I).

The first Regional Centre in Andhra Pradesh was started at Hyderabad on April 24, 1959, marked the beginning of the implementation of Workers' Education Scheme in Andhra Pradesh. Two more Regional Centres – one at Visakhapatnam and the other at Vijayawada were started during 1964 and 1974, respectively. All the 26 districts of Andhra Pradesh are covered by three Regional Centres. The Regional Centre and its activities are governed and guided by an Advisory Committee constituted for the purpose.

Regional Advisory Committees are constituted with the representatives of trade union organisations, managements, educational institutions and the State Governments. The Advisory Committees guide the functioning of the Regional Centres and perform the following functions:

— review the progress of the Scheme at regular intervals;
— recommend measures, as and when considered necessary, for proper implementation of the Programme of Workers' Education;
— seek and secure co-operation from employers and trade union organisations for the implementation of the Scheme;
— select candidates for admission to worker teacher courses;
— evaluate the worker teacher trainees at the conclusion of their training;
— approve books for addition to libraries at the regional and unit level;
— appoint sub-committees for the conduct of different businesses.

The Regional Centre at Hyderabad was started in the year 1959. It covers an area comprising 9 districts of Andhra Pradesh (Hyderabad, Rangareddy, Medak, Mahaboobnagar, Nalgonda, Warangal, Adilabad and Nizamabad) with no sub-regional centres. It covers both the public and private sector undertakings of the region.

The Vijayawada Regional Centre which hitherto acted as sub-regional centre was elevated as third regional centre in Andhra Pradesh on May 10, 1974. The industrial units and workers of Krishna, Guntur and Prakasam districts directly come under the regional centres itself whereas Nellore, Chittoor, Cuddapah, Kurnool and Anantapur districts' industrial units' an workers associate with the sub-regional centre at Tirupati which was closed subsequently.

The Visakhapatnam Regional Centre was started on 1-3-1964. The industrial units and workers of Visakhapatnam, Vizianagaram and Srikakulam directly come under the Visakhapatnam Region. East Godavari and West Godavari districts were covered by sub-regional centre at Rajahmundry and was closed subsequently. Since 1980, the centre has trained 591 Worker Teachers and 19,287 workers at Unit Level Classes (Table 2.3) approximately.

The Visakhapatnam Regional Centre organises the following programmes for the benefit of different categories of workers:

Regional level:

Three-month Worker Teacher Training Course

One month Leadership Development Course

Two-month Rural Workers' Education Course

One week Refresher Course for Worker Teachers

One week Orientation Course for Rural Educators

Three-day Joint Education Programmes for Workers and Management representatives on participation, productivity, safety etc.

Two-day Need-based seminars

Unit Level:

Three months part-time Unit Level Classes/3 weeks full-time ULC

Six months part-time Functional Adult Literacy Classes

One week need-based special programme

Two-day joint educational programme for members of shop councils, joint councils etc., at enterprise level.

Unorganised Sector:

Five-day camp for workers of small scale industries and unorganised sector

Two-day special programmes in collaboration with rural and tribal development agencies.

Achievements of the centre can be summarised as follows: Workers' Education has earned the goodwill of all the concerned. The centre has been recognised as the right agency to deliver goods; helped trade unions to have their own cadre of trainers and motivators to take up Workers' Education and organisational activity. Most of the Trade Unions functioning in the industrial units of this Region have trained Worker Teachers and those trained in Leadership Development Programmes as their office bearers and activities.

The industrial units of both public sector and private sectors covered by the Visakhapatnam Regional Centre are delineated in Appendix VI.

The total Worker Teachers and workers trained in ULCs in the Andhra Pradesh through its three Regional Centres, during the last 11 years was shown in Table 2.2 and the contribution of Visakhapatnam Region was shown in Table 2.3.

The public sector in India occupied a commanding position in the industrial sector which is a fountain head of socio-economic revolution and the champion of social justice. The phenomenal growth of the public sector can be accounted from the fact that the number of public sector undertakings has raised from 5 at the commencement of Five Year Plan to 1976 at the end of the 1979-80. The growth of investment also increased from Rs.29 crores in 1952 to Rs.15,602 crores in 1979-80.[8] Realising the importance of public sector, the VII Plan provides a total outlay of Rs.1,80,000 crores as against Rs.1,54,218 crores during the VI Plan.[9]

Table—2.2

Training of the Worker Teachers (Trainers) and Workers in Andhra Pradesh from 1980-2003

Year	*Worker Teachers (Trainers)*			*Workers (ULC)*		
	Public Sector	*Private Sector*	*Total*	*Public Sector*	*Private Sector*	*Total*
1980-81	330	24	354	7014	8166	15180
1981-82	322	27	349	5768	7474	13242
1982-83	270	30	300	4510	6315	10825
1983-84	223	13	236	4051	6399	10450
1984-85	NA	NA	NA	NA	NA	NA
1985-86	239	18	257	4036	6507	10543
1986-87	35	47	82	3625	852	4467
1987-88	NA	NA	NA	NA	NA	NA
1988-89	78	4	82	2842	891	3733
1989-90	98	7	105	4519	785	5294
1990-91	103	2	105	3018	411	3429
1991-92						
1992-93						
1993-94						
1994-95			-Not Available-			
1995-96						
1996-97						
1997-98						
1998-99	34	–	34	1542	400	1942
1999-2000	–	–	44	1434	447	1881
2000-2001	24	–	24	651	230	881
2001-2002	38	3	41	358	300	658
2002-2003	28	–	28	693	240	933

NA = not available (reoriented after Annual Reports of C.B.W.E.)

Table—2.3

Training of the Worker Teachers (Trainers) and workers in Visakhapatnam Region from 1980-2003

	Worker Teachers (Trainers)			*Workers (ULC)*		
Year	*Public Sector*	*Private Sector*	*Total*	*Public Sector*	*Private Sector*	*Total*
1980-81	95	7	102	2349	489	2838
1981-82	77	7	84	2354	714	3068
1982-83	92	7	99	1555	641	2196
1983-84	58	1	59	1095	1022	2117
1984-85	47	–	47	910	1146	2056
1985-86	50	6	56	887	1214	2161
1986-87	14	–	14	425	330	786
1987-88	22	–	22	835	156	991
1988-89	23	–	23	567	40	607
1989-90	24	3	27	544	125	669
1990-91	13	–	13	713	283	996
1991-92						
1992-93						
1993-94						
1994-95			-Not Available-			
1995-96						
1996-97						
1997-98						
1998-99	–	–	–	271	40	311
1999-2000	25	–	25	331	60	391
2000-2001	–	–	–	40	60	100
2001-2002	20	–	20	–	60	60
2002-2003	–	–	–	–	–	–

NA = not available (reoriented after Annual Reports of C.B.W.E. and Regional Centre, Visakhapatnam)

The public sector undertakings in Andhra Pradesh account for more than 70% of the fixed capital of the factory sector in the state. Visakhapatnam hosts a good number of mega-industries in the public sector of Andhra Pradesh. The classified list of public sector undertakings of Visakhapatnam is shown in Appendix VI.

Private sector investment in the VII Plan accounts for Rs.1,66,148 crores and is a prima facie evidence of the Indian Government stand on the private sector expansion.[10] It is also remembered particularly in the Indian context, "when there exist in the same industry both privately and public owned industries, it would continue to be the policy of the Indian Government to give a fair non-discriminatory treatment to both of them".[11]

The Government of Andhra Pradesh is also committed to give big boost to various basic industries – cement, paper, sugar, jute, mining, iron & steel, textiles etc., under private sector commensurate to the aspirations of the country's industrial policy. Among four regions (Rayalaseema, Coastal Andhra, Hyderabad including Telangana and Visakhapatnam Regions) in the State, Hyderabad and Visakhapatnam Regions assume greater importance in the development of basic and core industries.

Visakhapatnam region with its vast infrastructure facilities signaled for tremendous industrial growth during the present Century. Besides various industries under public sector, Visakhapatnam is a citadel for industrial development has attracted different types of industrial units under private sector too. Some of the major industrial units under private sector in the Visakhapatnam Region were shown in Appendix VI. They play a significant role in the fields of investment production, trade and labour.

So far, there has not been any study on the performance of Workers' Education Scheme in Visakhapatnam Region, which in the recent times has assumed increasing importance with its rapid industrialisation. Hence, the present study was undertaken with a view to assessing the impact of Workers' Education Scheme based on the first hand information. The study, its scope and objectives were delineated in Chapter III.

REFERENCES

1. Peterson Florence, *American Labour Unions,* Sterling Publishers Pvt., Ltd., New Delhi, 1952, p. 137.

2. Ramanujam, G., *A Peep into the Future in the Silver Jubilee Souvenir,* C.B.W.E., 1983, pp.19-20, (Former Chairman, C.B.W.E.)

3. Anjaiah, T., *Inaugural Address*, 83rd meeting of governing body of C.B.W.E., Govt. of India, 6th February, 1985 at New Delhi.

4. *Report of the Royal Commission on Labour*, 1931, p. 27.

5. Chansarkar, M.A., *Twenty Five Years in the Cause of Workers' Education*, Silver Jubilee Souvenir, C.B.W.E., 1983, p. 4.

6. *Ramanujam Committee* (Workers' Education Review Committee) Report, 1975 (accepted by the Board and the Govt. of India).

7. The Construction of Syllabi, *Labour Education*, 1983/3, ILO, Geneva, pp. 39 and 41.

8. Indian Labour Statistics, 1979, p. 316.

9. *The Hindu*, Monday, November 11, 1985, p. 6.

10. *The Hindu*, Monday, November 11, 1985, p. 6.

11. Third Five Year Plan draft report.

3

AIMS AND OBJECTIVES OF THE STUDY

Workers' Education Programme in India, is now in its youth, in most parts of the country. Very few have ever voluntarily attempted to examine the performance of the programme. During the first decade of its inception, several reports were available on the scope and functioning of the programme.

Charles A. Orr, the representative of the International Labour Organisation reviewed the scheme,[1] which was then practically in its infancy and advised the Government of India on:

1. establishing Central, Regional and State Workers' Education Boards;
2. implementing the teacher-administrators (now called Education Officers) training projects;
3. conducting demonstration projects such as courses and seminars;
4. assisting in the preparation of educational materials, audio-visual aids, etc., and
5. advising trade unions, at their request on Workers' Education Programme.

In the document of the 3rd Five Year Plan, the then Government had widely appreciated the scheme, as it had helped in developing the self confidence of workers to an appreciable extent. Further, in 1962, Mr.McNamara, Chief, Labour Division, USAID surveyed the Workers' Education Scheme and observed that the Workers'

Education Scheme was a large scale co-operative venture between Government, employers and trade unions.

In another study made by Hopkins, he opined that, though the role of C.B.W.E. was appreciable, the Workers' Education Programme was lacking spontaneity and responsiveness.

Apart from these reviews, several evaluations were made by different committees. The National Commission on Labour, appointed by the Government of India, submitted an evaluative report on the Scheme in November 1967. The Commission had the benefit of the reaction of the Board to its recommendations. These were further considered by the Commission and weighed against the direct evidence received by it in the area of Workers' Education. The Commissions' observations and recommendations were published as the "Report of the Committee on Workers' Education".[2]

In 1971, the Government of India appointed an Estimate Committee of the Parliament, pursuant to one of the recommendations made by this Committee, constituted in July, 1974. The purpose of the Committee was to evaluate the Workers' Education Scheme. The Chairperson of this committee was Sri G.Ramanujam, the General Secretary of the Indian National Trade Union Congress. The Committee submitted its report to the Government on July 20, 1975, but the report had not been made public as of August, 1977, and the findings of the committee were completely confidential.

The Board, with the aid of its own Education Officers, conducted sixteen diagnostic studies in selected industrial undertakings. These studies, all of which were conducted before, 1970, were evaluative and threw light on specific industries. There had also been a regional study confined to the Bombay area made by a sub-committee set up by the Scheme's Regional Centre at Bombay.

All the reviews and evaluations mentioned so far had been conducted by the Committees appointed by the Government of India or by members of the Board who were also Governmental personnel.

Gandhi[3] had studied the Workers' Education Scheme in India, and its implementation. Her studies though not exhaustive have delineated and emphasized the importance for the extension of such studies in other regions also, so as to assess the Scheme considering regional variations. Mahar[4] also had made a critical study of Workers' Education Scheme in India with special reference to its role in Government Presses. The study has evidently demonstrated the fact that the problems of Workers' Education Schemes vary from one type of industry to another and stressed the need for modifying the Programme according to the needs of workers in different types of industry. Sivapalan[5] has made a good study–An enquiry into the Workers' Education Programmes in Kerala with a view to suggest improvements.

Kakkar[6] studied comprehensively the Workers' Education in India. Virmani[7] carried out research on Workers' Education in 1989. Special case studies were made by several people from different regions on various aspects of Workers' Education. Reddy[8] studied the performance requirements of Workers Teachers as perceived by Workers Teachers of Workers' Education Centres. Kanthamma[9] inquired into the facilities available to the industrial workers in Cuddapah district. Bhasha[10] studied the attitude of workers towards Workers' Education Programme in Chittoor district. However, these studies were mostly unpublished. Buch[11] surveyed the Research in Education wherein he dealt with the Research Programmes related to Workers' Education.

In spite of several evaluations and reviews, so far no information exists on to what extent the actual objectives of the Workers' Education Programmes are realised. The C.B.W.E. has seven objectives ultimately leading to the take over of Workers' Education Programme by the trade unions. Now the questions is, whether these objectives have been realised or not? If so, to what extent? Answering to these questions may help in either to streamline the Programme or to review the approach adopted and its effectiveness.

The present study is an attempt to examine the Workers' Education Programme in different types of industries and to contribute the information that helps in the evaluation and assessment of the Programmes' impact. The main objectives of the study are:

1. to evaluate and assess the effect of the Workers' Education Schemes on the development of healthy mental attitude to work discipline, productivity, leadership and the intelligent participation of workers in social and economic development of the nation.
2. to assess the degree of participation of industrial units in the Workers' Education Scheme;
3. to identify the problems involved in implementing Workers' Education Schemes:
4. to suggest the ways and measures to adopt the different levels – government, industry, trade union etc., to make the Workers' Education more purposeful and
5. to review the achievements of the Workers' Education Programmes.

Seven types of major industries of Visakhapatnam Region were selected for the present study. Of these, Visakhapatnam Port Trust (VPT), Dock Labour Board (DLB), Bharat Heavy Plate & Vessels Limited (BHPV) of Visakhapatnam belong to the Public Sector while Ferro Alloys Corporation (FACOR), Shreeramnagar, Nellimerla Jute Mills Ltd., (NJM), Nellimerla, Andhra Pradesh Paper Mills Ltd., (APPM), Rajahmundry, an Sri Ramadas Motor Transport Limited (SRMT), Kakinada, belonged to the private sector.

The approach to the study and the methods adopted were delineated in the Chapter IV and the data analysis and inferences were described and discussed from Chapter V.

REFERENCES

1. Report to the Government of India on Workers' Education, ILO's Office (regular programmes of technical assistance), ILO, Geneva, 1960.
2. Report of the National Commission on Labour, Workers' Education, Manager of Publications, Delhi, 1967, p.52.
3. Gandhi Kalyani, *The Workers' Education Scheme of India*, Doctoral Thesis, The State University of New Jersey, U.S.A., 1979.
4. Mahar Allah, *A Critical study of Workers' Education Scheme in India with Special Reference to their Role in Government of India Presses*, Doctoral Thesis, Aligarh Muslim University, Aligarh, 1979.

5. Sivapalan, T.R. Unnithan, *An Enquiry into the Workers' Education Programme in Kerala with a View to Suggest Improvements*, Doctoral Thesis, University of Kerala, Trivandrum, 1990.

6. Kakkar, N.K., *Workers' Education in India*, Sterling Publishers (Pvt.) Ltd., New Delhi, 1973.

7. Virmani, B.R., *Workers' Education*, B.R. Administrative Staff College of India, Hyderabad, 1989.

8. Reddy, M.M., *The Performance Requirements of Worker Teachers as Perceived by Worker Teachers of Workers' Education Centres*, Doctoral Thesis, S.V.University, Tirupati, 1987.

9. Kanthamma, K. *The Facilities Available to the Industrial Workers in Cuddapah District*, M.Phil. Dissertation, S.V. University, Tirupati, 1986.

10. Bhasha Khadar, *The Attitude of Workers towards Workers' Education Programme in Chittoor District*, Doctoral Thesis, S.V. University, Tirupati, 1981.

11. Buch, M.B. *Third Survey of Research in Education*, NCERT, New Delhi, 1986, p.1004.

PART—II

METHODOLOGY

The present study on the Impact of Workers' Education in selected public and private sector undertakings of Visakhapatnam region was carried out. The selected public and private sector undertakings in the study were listed in Chapter III and the criteria for selecting these industries was based on the method of representative samples like rural and urban based industries; multiple and single union industries; technically oriented and non-technical industries etc. Thus, ensuring a heterogeneous structural representation; sample consists of large, medium and small sized industrial units whose work force ranged from below 1000 to 12000. Incidentally, they represented three of the four districts of the Central Board for Workers' Education of Visakhapatnam Region.

Since the aim of the study is to evaluate the impact of Workers' Education Scheme, the basic approach followed to measure the impact was direct inventory method. The data was collected directly from various people involved in the scheme, and were classified into five groups:

- *(a)* Worker Trainees in ULCs
- *(b)* Worker Teachers (Trainers)
- *(c)* Trade Unions
- *(d)* Managements
- *(e)* Education Officers of CBWE

The strength of the Worker Trainees in ULCs and Worker Teachers in relation to the workforce in the industry and the percentage covered by sampling were delineated in Table 4.1.

Table—4.1

Percentage sample of Worker Teachers (Trainers) and Worker Trainees (ULC) in relation to their strength in the industry and the total workforce

Industry	*Total Workforce*	*Total WTs*	*% Questioned*	*% Responded*	*Total Workers (ULC)*	*% Questioned*	*% Responded*
VPT	12,000	141	82.27	22.70	5,089	2.67	0.79
DLB	3,500	.38	84.21	57.89	568	9.51	0.70
BHPV	4,247	44	68.18	18.18	290	15.17	12.41
FACOR	5,000	8	100.00	87.50	1,083	6.28	0.37
NJM	6,098	8	100.00	100.00	2,290	6.90	0.61
APPM	7,000	6	100.00	50.00	261	22.22	0.00
SRMT	6,000	6	100.00	83.33	100	22.00	0.00
Over all %			33.61	13.87		5.58	1.01

The inventory can be conveniently described under seven phases, which includes secondary data collection phase, questionnaire phase, personal observations phase, personal interviews phase, academic phase, review phase and analysis phase.

In order to understand the Workers' Education Scheme, its implementation and progress, and also to provide sound base for the direct inventory, during the first phase, all published reports, documents, books and other material were scanned and a base of the secondary data was established. The source of the secondary data includes periodical reports of the CBWE, research papers and documents of earlier similar studies comprehensive books, journals of CBWE and the periodical publications of the ILO, Geneva. Besides, certain statistical information was obtained from the relevant industries and CBWE.

The questionnaire and personal observation phase were simultaneously proceeded with. Detailed questionnaires were developed for various people involved in the scheme. The questionnaires so developed were appended as: Appendix-VII for Worker Teachers (Trainers), Appendix-VIII for Worker Trainees and Appendix-IX for Trade Union representatives. The sequence of questions in the questionnaire for Worker Teachers and Worker Trainees was so arranged to indicate the personal affiliation of the questionee, his faith in the scheme, his opinion on functioning of the scheme under their unions', managements' jurisdictions; impact on the person; lacunae and remedies.

The questionnaires were developed in the regional language, Telugu and in case where the questionee happened to be a non-Telugu speaking person, such persons were assisted by oral translation and results were recorded on the questionnaires accordingly. Although a good number of people from each group were available to involve in the survey, greater effort was made to convince the target groups to make them accept the questionnaire. Recovery of the circulated questionnaires needed special efforts and the information and the degree of effort made to recover the questionnaire from each of the questionee, was used to express the motivation required by the questionee which indirectly indicated the general interest and awareness level of the sample in the scheme. After the recovery of the questionnaire, the individuals were made to enter into a brief discussion, wherein some questions either related to those in the questionnaire, or those that most of the people hesitate to answer in writing. Some of these questions helped in the indirect assessment of the some of the study's objectives (Appendix – X).

Necessary care has been taken to involve all the age groups and professional groups' personnel. The number of visits made to each questionee to recover the questionnaire was considered as the effort placed on it.

Simultaneously, with the questionnaire phase, personal observations of the author on the implementation and functioning of the scheme in the respective industries were recorded systematically by verifying an improvised check-list specially developed for the purpose. The check-list includes a variety of aspects like the number of functioning ULCs, attendance in the ULCs, attitude of different unions to this scheme, reading material available to the Worker Teachers , reading material provided to worker trainees, leadership attitude of the individuals, teaching methods adopted by Worker Teachers , involvement of worker trainees in ULCs etc. The data so recorded and obtained was used to confirm certain facts expressed by various questionees.

The next phase involves personal interviews especially with the respective managements of industries and the Education Officers of CBWE dealing with the Workers' Education Scheme in the region. As in the personal observations phase, for the personal interviews also a detailed and improvised check-list was developed which is flexible and can be modified and attuned to the prevailing situation in the concerned industries. The check-list developed to interview the management representatives included aspects like management's support to the Workers' Education Scheme, facilities provided to the Workers' Education Scheme by the management, opinion on the functioning of Workers' Education Scheme in their industry, interest and faith in Workers Education Scheme and lacunae and remedies for a better Workers' Education Scheme. The response of the management to the present study was poor which by itself is considered the management's attitude towards the scheme. The check-list developed for the Education Officers of CBWE covers diversed aspects ranging from financial grants released for the scheme, efficiency of the mechanism, three-tier training, material being developed for worker teachers and worker trainees, participation in the ULCs, feed-back procedure adopted by CBWE etc.

Academic phase constitutes discussions and gathering of the opinions of the educationists, sociologists and social scientists were collected on:

(i) The impact of Workers' Education Scheme

(ii) Relevance of the syllabi

(iii) Mechanism of implementation and

(iv) Efficiency of the present approach etc.

The above elitists were provided access to the data collected in the first four phases, so as to equip them for better diagnosis. The opinions of the group were recorded systematically, so as to design the review phase, in which any missing information or lacunae in the primary or secondary data obtained were attended to. Further, the opinions of the above elitists helped in the aspect of suggesting changes in the present Scheme for Workers' Education.

In the review phase, based on the interviews with the actual people involved in the Workers' Education Scheme and long discussions with academicians of different fields a detailed data-review-programme was designed to repeat and modify any of the above phases in respect of certain individuals or groups, in case, if any vital information was left unanswered or not questioned or not included in the actual programme.

Methods suitable to those adopted in the earlier phase were adopted to repeat and review any facet of inventory. This helped in completing the gaps if any, in the inventory, subject to the limitations of the study and study programme.

The final phase was 'analysis' phase in which data collected or obtained from various sources and personnel were analysed to realise the objectives of the present study. Mostly, all respondents and reactions were expressed in terms of proportional unit or percentage. For the convenience of readers, the tabulated data contained numbers and percentage, in most of the cases and wherever is possible.

Appropriate statistical techniques were adopted to find out relationships, if any, between any of the variables, for which the standard methods of line equations were used.

Although the methods adopted in the study and approach followed were of standard procedures prescribed for such studies, the study has its own limitations beyond the control of the author and were delineated below.

1. The sample drawn from different groups varies in size from industry to industry which largely depended upon the size of the work force of the industry;
2. A great time lapse occurred between circulation of the questionnaire and their recovery. In most cases, the recovery was not possible and another questionnaire was served to the same or different individual; This difficult process and task has greatly influenced the sample size especially in the industries with a large workforce;
3. The attitude of the groups involved in the scheme, was mostly different and the continuous insistence for realising the survey formalities must have influenced some of the details expressed by questionees. However, personal interviews with such persons were essentially held so as to confirm their reflections;
4. The programme has not been sponsored or financed by any agency or the institutions while the finances required for making a single visit to all seven industries would cost around Rs.1,000/- and the distance to be travelled would be around 700 km. Thus, financial constraints played a vital role in improving the recovery rate of the questionnaire so as to have a greater size of the sample; and
5. Since most of the industries and unions, CBWE centres or any other government agencies, related to Labour or Labour Welfare do not have any concrete feed-back

system, they were not able to maintain detailed statistics or information based on CBWE Scheme. Thus, past data on Workers' Education Scheme, either industry-wise or at Unit level Class level, was not available for reference.

6. In order to make the study suitable for a comparison with other studies (on-going and completed) in different regions of the country, more ethnographic methods have been adopted as those methods are suitable to employ in a majority of the Indian situation.

5

ANALYSIS AND INFERENCES

Profile and Response

The sample selected for the study, represents a cross section of the Industries and Unions of Visakhapatnam Region, three industries from Public Sector and four from Private Sector. All the three Public Sector industries were located at Visakhapatnam City, while four Private Sector industries, Ferro Alloys Corporation (FACOR) and Nellimerla Jute Mills Ltd., (NJM) were located at rural centres, and the areas of Andhra Pradesh Paper Mills Limited (APPM) and Sri Ramadas Motor Transport Limited (SRMT) can be considered as urban centres. In spite of the types of location, a majority of the workforce in these industries hail from rural regions. However, the workers at urban centres are rather urbanised. The total workforce in all these seven industries was well over 45,000 to whom the Workers' Education Programme is intended to, and relevant.

Industries and Unions

All the seven industries have well organised trade unions, ranged in number from 1 to 5 recognised unions in each industry. However, all the industries have a single dominating union (Table 5.1).

Of the total seven dominating unions, A.I.T.U.C., I.N.T.U.C., H.M.S., and B.M.S., are central unions and they exist in many other industries also.

In two of the private sector industries i.e., NJM and SRMT, there was only one recognised union. However, in NJM, the union was affiliated to I.N.T.U.C., while in SRMT, it was an independent union.

Table—5.1

Workforce and union strength in different industries

Industry	*Total Workforce (approx.)*	*Dominating Union*	*Union strength (% of total workforce)*
VPT	12,000	H.M.S.	65.00
DLB	3,500	H.M.S.	54.29
BHPV	4,247	B.M.S.	67.74
FACOR	5,000	B.M.S.	79.92
NJM	6,098	I.N.T.U.C.	100.00
APPM	7,000	A.I.T.U.C.	56.06
SRMT	6,000	S.R.M.T.E.U.	100.00

VPT = Visakhapatnam Port Trust; DLB = Dock Labour Board; FACOR = Ferro Alloys Corporation; NJM = Nellimerla Jute Mills Ltd.; APPM = Andhra Pradesh Paper Mills Ltd.; SRMT = Sri Ramadas Motor Transport Ltd.

All efforts have been made to involve all the existing unions in the present study. However, some of the unions whose membership, activity and affairs were at a very low key, were reluctant to participate and respond. However, it can be assumed that their participation in the Workers' Education Programme also would be proportionately low and can no way significantly affect the results of the present study.

The attitudes of various groups, i.e., management, trade unions, Worker Teachers and workers towards the Workers' Education Programme can be indirectly gauged by the quantum of response received from them to this study.

Managements

Of the nine top managerial personnel with whom interviews were tried, only two have responded fairly, while others have either directed to their subordinates or spared no time. Incidentally the two employers who responded were from the private sector.

In the public sector, personnel at middle management level also have responded similar to their top management counterparts. However, the personnel at middle management level in the Private Sector, extended reasonable co-operation.

Trade Unions

The response from trade union leaders was comparatively poor, the reason being, their availability was rare and often it is difficult to meet the individuals as their programmes varied highly. Of the 21 members who accepted the questionnaire, only 13 have duly responded. Of the 21 personnel belonging to 16 unions, only 13 members of seven unions have responded. I.N.T.U.C. was the only union, from which the response has come from three industries followed by A.I.T.U.C. from two industries. The affiliation of the members responded was shown in the Table 5.2.

Table—5.2

Representation of different unions in the sample

	VPT	*DLB*	*BHPV*	*FACOR*	*NJM*	*APPM*	*SRMT*	*Total*
I.N.T.U.C.	1	–	–	1	2	–	–	4
A.I.T.U.C.	1	–	–	–	–	1	–	2
H.M.S.	2	–	–	–	–	–	–	2
B.M.S.	–	–	–	–	–	–	–	0
Others	–	–	2 (NEU)	–	–	1	2	5
Total	4	0	2	1	2	2	2	13

The response of Worker Teachers was very high in the private sector, while that of workers it was from the public sector. The high response of Worker Teachers at private sector, however, has the unknown impact of the low number of Worker Teachers trained there. Among public sector units, DLB Worker Teachers responded fairly high. Nearly 29% of the Worker Teachers in the public sector units were not willing to accept the questionnaires and evaded by some or other reasons (Table 5.3).

Table—5.3

Response of Worker Teachers (Trainers) and workers in different industries

Industry	*Worker Teachers (Trainers)*		*Workers (ULC)*	
	Questioned	*Responded*	*Questioned*	*Responded*
VPT	116	32 (27.59)	136	40 (29.41)
DLB	32	22 (68.75)	54	04 (7.41)
BHPV	30	08 (26.67)	44	36 (81.82)
FACOR	08	07 (87.50)	68	04 (5.88)
NJM	08	08 (100.00)	158	14 (8.86)
APPM	06	03 (50.00)	58	0
SRMT	06	05 (83.33)	22	0
Total	**206**	**85 (41.26)**	**540**	**98 (18.15)**

Figures in parenthesis are respective percentages

Of the 206 Worker Teachers (Trainers) who accepted the questionnaire, seven Worker Teachers have returned them in time and without any further visits. 78 have returned only after motivation of varying degrees as shown below. Thus, total responded was accounted for 41.26% of the Worker Teachers who accepted the questionnaire (Table 5.4).

Table—5.4

Response of Worker Teachers in public and private sectors to different degrees of motivation

Degree of Motivation	*Public Sector*	*Private Sector*
Little Motivation	2 (3.64)	3 (13.04)
Moderate Motivation	14 (25.45)	8 (34.78)
High Motivation	39 (70.91)	12 (52.17)

Figures in parenthesis are respective percentages

On the other hand, only one out of every 20 workers requested, have accepted the questionnaire, but a little above 18% returned the same. The motivation required by the workers to return the duly answered questionnaires id delineated in Table 5.5.

Table—5.5

Response of workers to different degrees of motivation

Degree of Motivation	*Public Sector*	*Private Sector*
Little Motivation	15 (18.75)	9 (50.00)
Moderate Motivation	22 (27.50)	4 (22.22)
High Motivation	43 (53.75)	5 (27.78)

Figures in parenthesis are respective percentages

The interest of the Worker Teachers and workers, in the Workers' Education Programme and its improvement, can be indirectly measured through their response to the present study. Further, the effect of motivation on realising the response is evident from Fig.5.1.

It is most surprising and unfortunate that the workers who attended Unit Level Classes in two industries, namely, APPM and SRMT, have not responded even to a high degree of motivation.

AFFILIATION, STRUCTURE AND COMPOSITION OF WORKFORCE

Worker Teachers (Trainers)

The Worker Teachers (Trainers) who responded, belonged to both Public and Private Sector undertakings and various dominant trade unions. Thus, the views of the respondents reflect the views of various types of industries and unions belonging to both public and private sectors. The affiliation of Worker Teachers to various unions is shown in Table 5.6.

Some of the unions (Table 5.6) were not affiliated to any of the central trade unions, but were affiliated to local district unions. It is most unfortunate to record that none of the female Worker Teachers were neither active nor responded. Thereby, the response was biased towards male community. However, this will not have any bearing on the study, since none of the women Worker Teachers have even handled the Unit Level Classes or doing so till to date.

Table—5.6

Composition of the responded Worker Teachers belonging to different unions and industries

Name of the Industry	*Union Affiliation*	*Number of respondents*	
Visakhapatnam Port Trust, Visakhapatnam	H.M.S.	20	
	A.I.T.U.C.	6	32
	I.N.T.U.C.	6	
Dock Labour Board, Visakhapatnam	I.N.T.U.C.	2	
	A.I.T.U.C.	2	22
	*N.E.U.	18	
Bharat Heavy Plate & Vessels Ltd., Visakhapatnam	*N.E.U.	8	8
Ferro Alloys Corporation, Shreeramnagar	B.M.S.	5	7
	I.N.T.U.C.	2	
Nellimerla Jute Mills, Nellimerla	I.N.T.U.C.	8	8
Andhra Pradesh Paper Mills Ltd., Rajahmundry	*F.I.T.U.C.	1	
	A.I.T.U.C	1	3
	I.N.T.U.C.	1	
Sri Ramadas Motor Transport, Kakinada	*S.R.M.T. Employees Union	5	5
Total		**85**	**85**

* Not a centrally affiliated union

Through the response received from Worker Teachers, different aspects which help in the assessment of the impact of Workers' Education Programme were analysed and finally the impact of the programme in realising the basic objectives in the views of Worker Teachers was delineated.

At the outset, the profile, and the affiliation of the Worker Teachers were explained. 72% of them belonged to two age groups between 26 and 45 years, and with a services of more than eleven years but below 30 years (Table 5.7).

Table—5.7

Age-service groups of Worker Teachers responded

Age groups	*Service in years*				*Total*
	Below 10	*11-20*	*21-30*	*31 and above*	
Below 25	2	–	–	–	2
26–35	3	25	2	–	30
36–45	–	13	22	–	35
46–55	–	1	9	5	15
56 and above	–	–	–	3	3
Total	**5**	**39**	**33**	**8**	**85**

The Worker Teachers aged above 46 years and more than 20 years of service in the industry constituted only a little more than 20%. In fact, this aged and experienced group of people have high influence over the worker learners and also in handling the classes for adult employed learners. Regrettably, this group is a small fraction of the Worker Teachers ' community.

The basic educational qualifications, cadre, role in different administrative committees, role in the trade union etc., have a great bearing on the status of Worker Teachers and as well influence their functioning limitations and relations with workers, thirty per cent of the Worker Teachers have education beyond higher secondary level. The rest of the 70% were below secondary level and the difference in the educational qualifications of these Worker Teachers and the worker learners is very limited and in all probability affect the student-teacher relationship in the class (Table 5.8).

Table—5.8

Educational qualifications of worker-teachers

Educational qualifications	*Number*	*Percentage*
Illiterates	–	–
Below Primary level	–	–
Primary level	13	15.29
Secondary level	47	55.30
Higher Secondary level	25	29.41

With regard to the cadre of Worker Teachers , majority (50.58%) belonged to technical personnel followed by clerical (42.35%) and others constituted 7.07% (Table 5.9).

Table—5.9

Representation of worker-teachers belonging to different types of jobs

Nature of job	*Number*	*Percentage*
Technical	43	50.58
Non-technical	1	1.17
Clerical	36	42.35
Class IV	5	5.90

Some of the Worker Teachers have acquired additional responsibilities of being members of different committees in the industry, like Canteen Committee, Safety Committee, Co-operative Committee etc. Their proportional representation was shown in Table 5.10. Nearly 42.39% of Worker Teachers were not involved in any of these special committees.

Table—5.10

Additional responsibilities obtained by some of the Worker Teachers

S. No.	*Name of the Committee*	*Number*	*Percentage*
1.	Canteen Committee	16	18.82
2.	Safety Committee	14	16.47
3.	Works Committee	13	15.29
4.	Others		
	(a) Co-operative Stores Committee	1	1.17
	(b) Sports Committee	1	1.17
	(c) SRMT Credit Society Committee	1	1.17
	(d) P.F. Trust Committee	3	3.52

It is stressed that more than 74% of Worker Teachers who are mere members of their trade unions while the rest held different posts in the executive body of the concerned unions (Table 5.11).

Table—5.11

Positions of Worker Teachers in their unions

Position	*Number*	*Percentage*
General Secretary	6	7.06
Joint Secretary	10	11.77
Secretary	–	–
Executive Members	6	7.06
Members	63	74.11

A good number (44.70%) of Worker Teachers were active members of political parties while another 36.47% were supporters of various parties. Thus, the ideologies of Worker Teachers in all probability were influenced by the ideologies of various political parties and unions (Table 5.12).

Table—5.12

Degrees of involvement in politics by Worker Teachers

Degree of involvement	*Number*	*Percentage*
Active	38	44.70
Supporter	31	36.47
No Politics	16	18.83

With regard to the background of Worker Teachers, 56.65% of them hail from rural areas and 58.82% of them belong to socially backward castes (Table 5.13). Of the socially backward castes, 16.00% belong to the Scheduled Castes, 2.00% belong to Scheduled Tribes and 82.00% belong to lower Backward Castes.

Table—5.13

Community and nativity backgrounds of Worker Teachers

Caste	*Nativity*			*Percentage*
	Rural	*Urban*	*Total*	
Scheduled Castes	5	3	8	9.41
Scheduled Tribes	1	-	1	1.18
Backward Castes	30	11	41	48.23
Other Castes	13	22	35	41.18
Total (percentage)	**49 (57.65)**	**36 (42.35)**		

Worker Learners (ULC) (Trainees)

A detailed analysis of the profile, affiliation and background of the workers attended the Unit Level Classes (ULC) was made so as to understand their levels of perception and consider the views expressed.

81.63% of the workers responded belonged to public sector, while 18.37% belonged to only 2 of 4 units in private sector. The following table delineates the workers attended the ULCs of different industries surveyed and their affiliation to different unions (Table 5.14).

Table—5.14

Union affiliation of workers responded in different industries

Industry	*Central Union*	*Number of respondents*		*Percentage*
VPT	H.M.S.	25		
	A.I.T.U.C.	8	40	40.82
	I.N.T.U.C.	7		
DLB	I.N.T.U.C.	1		
	A.I.T.U.C.	1	4	4.08
	*N.E.U.	2		
BHPV	*N.E.U.	36	36	36.73
Public Sector	**Total**	**80**	**80**	**81.63**
FACOR	B.M.S.	3		
	I.N.T.U.C.	1	4	4.08
NJM	I.N.T.U.C.	14		14.29
APPM	–	–		–
SRMT	–	–		–
Private Sector	**Total**	**18**	**18**	**18.37**

* Not a centrally affiliated union

A matrix for the age groups and service of the workers attended Unit Level Classes was shown in Table 5.15. According to which, more than 70% of the worker learners were between the ages 26 and 45 years and the service of less than 10 years. The rest of the 30% were distributed in another age group with more than 10 years of experience in the industry.

Table—5.15

Age-service groups of worker responded

Age groups	*Service in years*				
	Less than 10	*11-20*	*21-30*	*31 and above*	*Total (%)*
Below 25	4	–	2	–	6 (6.12)
26-35	50	2	4	2	58 (59.18)
36-45	20	2	2	–	24 (24.49)
46 and above	6	–	2	2	10 (10.21)
Total (Percentage)	5 (81.63)	4 (4.08)	10 (10.21)	4 (4.21)	

The matrix developed for the background of the workers was shown in the Table 5.16, and observed that more than 60% of the workers are having rural background while lower background, while lower Backward communities and the Forward castes dominated the scene and the representation of Scheduled Castes and Scheduled Tribes who are minimal. The distribution of workers with rural background would have been much more and the response from the private sector undertakings is greater.

Table—5.16

Community and nativity background of workers

Caste	*Nativity*			*Percentage*
	Rural	*Urban*	*Total*	
Scheduled Castes	6	8	14	14.28
Scheduled Tribes	–	2	2	2.04
Backward Castes	32	4	36	36.74
Other Castes	2[illegible]	24	46	46.94
Total (percentage)	60 (61.22)	38 (38.78)		

About 68% of the respondent workers, have only school education, of which nearly 1/3rd were below primary level of education only. Of the workers who have mere school education belonged to Lower Backward Classes (26%), Scheduled Castes (12%) and Scheduled Tribes (2%) while the remaining 28% belonged to Forward Communities.

A good number of (63.27%) of the workers attending Unit Level Classes were doing technical jobs. Other cadres which followed this group were mazdoors (14.29%), non-technical personnel (12.24%) and clerical (10.20%). Thus the composition of Worker Teachers and workers were broadly similar in having the technical personnel as dominant group (Table 5.17).

Table—5.17

Representation of workers belonging to different types of jobs

Designation	*Number*	*Percentage*
Technical	62	63.27
Non-technical	12	12.24
Clerical	10	10.20
Mazdoors (Labour)	14	14.29

Although, all the workers were having general membership in trade unions, they had never been a member of the executive of the union and their involvement in politics was relatively minimal.

ANALYSIS

Faith and Interest

As regards to faith in the Programme, the response varied from group to group. Management representatives in the public sector opined that the Programme did not enhance the educative levels of the workers but made workers more conscious of their rights than their duties. Management representatives of the private sector, were more realistic and expressed complete faith in the Programme on the condition that the direction of the Programme is regulated. The private sector managements opined that the implementation of the Programme wants of sincerely.

All the Worker Teachers and workers have expressed complete faith in the Programme. However, they complained of the rather diffused co-operation from all the sectors (management, trade unions and C.B.W.E.).

To evaluate the interests of Worker Teachers, the reasons for joining the Programmes and the motivation they received were examined. 54.12% of the Worker Teachers have joined voluntarily while the remaining have motivated by different individuals or unions. About 10.59% of the Worker Teachers joined in the interest of the union, while 23.53% have joined with an aim to participate in their community development. Table 5.18 delineates various reasons commonly expressed by the Worker Teachers for joining the Programme.

Table—5.18

Motivation received and types of interest of Worker Teachers, in joining the programme

Sl. No.	*Types of interest*	*Motivation*		*Percentage (%)*
		Voluntarily	*By others*	
1.	In the interest of the union	2	7	9 (10.59)
2.	Enthusiasm and Curiosity	9	3	12 (14.12)
3.	To have improved Social Relations	19	11	30 (35.29)
4.	To participate in the Community Development	11	9	20 (23.53)
5.	More than the above	5	9	14 (16.47)
	Total (percentage)	**46 (54.12)**	**39 (45.88)**	

To understand the interest of the workers in the Unit Level Classes of Workers' Education Programme, their interest and faith in joining the programme were considered and from Table 5.19 as was evident that the majority of the workers have joined the course to understand their rights and duties, welfare schemes and labour acts related to their job, while most of them were not interested on productivity or the industrial relations or safety.

On the faith, they have in the Scheme almost all the respondents expressed positivity, but were not keen as was evident from the information on their attending the classes and involvement in the class room work (Table 5.23 and 5.32). more than 65% of Worker Teachers complained irregular attendance or untimely attendance as one of the major problems in conduct of Unit Level Classes. It was also expressed that there were no stipulated rules for attendance and majority of workers consider it very casually, the main reason being the feeling of non-functional relationship of the Programme with their career.

Table—5.19

Subjects favoured by worker respondents to have in their curriculum

Subjects	*Number*	*Percentage*
Rights and duties	69	70.41
Labour Acts	58	59.18
Welfare Schemes	63	64.29
Industrial Relations	33	33.67
Safety	39	39.80
Productivity	27	27.55

The total number of Worker Teachers trained was very high in the public sector undertakings when compared to the private sector undertakings. However, percentage of teachers who were conducting classes was much greater in the private sector as was evident from the following table drawn from the respondents (Table 5.20).

Table—5.20

Inactive Worker Teachers of public and private sector industries

Sector	*Name of the Industry*	*Trained Worker Teachers*			
		Responded		*Not active*	
		n	%	*n*	%
Public	VPT	32	27.59	10	31.25
	DLB	22	68.75	14	63.64
	BHPV	8	26.67	8	100.00
	Total	**62**	**34.83**	**32**	**51.61**
Private	FACOR	7	87.50	1	14.29
	NJM	8	100.00	0	0
	APPM	3	50.00	0	0
	SRMT	5	100.00	5	100.00
	Total	**23**	**82.14**	**6**	**26.09**

An analysis of the age and designation of the inactive Worker Teachers revealed that though the age has no visible influence over the inactiveness of the above Worker Teachers , their cadre appears to have some bearing as was evident from the following table (Table 5.21). It is evident that clerical group was the first major group (as Worker Teachers from Class IV were very meagre) and surprisingly all the inactive Worker Teachers of Clerical grade were from the public sector. On the other hand, the technical cadre inactive Worker Teachers though appear to have equally distributed to public sector and private sectors, relatively at private sector they were more inactive (Table 5.21).

Table—5.21

Involvement of Worker Teachers of different age groups and designations

Status	*Worker Teachers*			
	Responded		*Not active*	
	N	*%*	*N*	*%*
Age-groups				
Below 25	2	100.00	0	0
26-35	30	45.45	16	53.33
36-45	35	38.04	16	45.71
46-55	15	37.50	6	40.00
56 and above	3	50.00	0	0
Designations				
Technical	43	41.34	18	41.86
Non-technical	1	25.00	0	0
Clerical	36	41.38	15	41.66
Class IV	5	45.45	5	100.00

According to Table 5.22, nearly one third of the Worker Teachers trained and responded were not conducting Unit Level Classes and were inactive and all of these inactive Worker Teachers belong to the classes of either not unsatisfied or unsatisfied (Table 5.37). The remaining Worker Teachers who were conducting Unit Level Classes have grouped into three classes based on the number of classes they organise per year. 20% of the total respondents conducts only one class a year, while 22.35% twice a year and 12.94% thrice a year with full schedule. Together, these groups accounts for 55.29% of total respondents.

Table—5.22

Frequency of the conduct of Unit Level Classes/year by individual worker teacher

Frequency	*Number*	*Percentage*
Once a year	17	20.00
Twice a year	19	22.35
Thrice a year	11	12.94
Inactive (not conducting any classes)	38	44.71

The interests of workers in Unit Level Classes and their enthusiasm to learn also reflect from their regularity in attending the Unit Level Classes. As discussed earlier, Worker Teachers expressed that the attendance in their classes has been a continuous problem (Table 5.24 and 5.32). The response from the workers on their irregularity in attending the classes revealed that the timings of the classes is not corresponding to the daily schedule of the learners especially in the industries where most of the workers work in different shifts based on which their daily schedule variously distributed. On the other hand, domestic responsibilities, tiresomeness etc., were common reasons for the poor attendance in Unit Level Classes (Table 5.23).

Table—5.23

Reasons expressed by workers for their irregularity

Reasons	*Number*	*Percentage*
Tiresomeness	18	18.37
Overtime work	34	34.69
Domestic works	24	24.49
Unsuitable timings	66	67.35

Various common problems encountered by the Worker Teachers in the conduct of classes have been explained in Table 5.24. Of these, learners' attendance, teaching aids, receiving guidance and availability of resource persons and the conduct of study tour were more prominent. 64.81% of the Worker Teachers expressed that regularity in the attendance of the learners is very poor and even those attended regularly were not time conscious in attending the classes to an extent of 68.23%. Nearly 63% of the Worker Teachers expressed that the guidance they receive from management or unions or from the C.B.W.E. is not upto the mark, while 84.70% of the Worker Teachers have problems in utilising the services of various resource persons from external agencies. 84.70% of the Worker Teachers were not conducting study tours for several reasons and emphasized the need for urgent action by the unions or managements or both (Table 5.24).

Table—5.24

Problems expressed by Worker Teachers in conducting the Unit Level classes

Sl. No.	*Common Problems*	*Number*	*Percentage*
1.	*(a)* Attendance	55	64.70
	(b) Timely attendance	58	68.23
2.	Use of Training aids/instruments	53	62.35
3.	Obtaining advice and correspondences from the Workers' Education Institutions and trade unions' co-operation	60	70.58
4.	Study tours	55	64.70

Conduct of Unit Level Classes

Topics of Interest. It was evident that majority of the Worker Teachers (70.58%) preferred topics on the Workers' Education and Industrial Relations. The next importance was given to History and Development of Trade Unions (61.17%) followed by Labour Laws (57.64%). All these high preferred topics were related to their rights and privileges (Table 5.25).

Regarding the Workers' Education Scheme, almost all the 85 respondents felt the need and utmost importance for Workers' Education while their preference to many of the topics related to the basic objectives of the programme, was low when compared to the topics of their personal interests such as those described above.

Table—5.25

Topics favoured by Worker Teachers to have in the curriculum for ULC

Descriptions	*Number*	*Percentage*
Workers' Education	60	70.58
Labour Laws	49	57.64
Trade Unions (History and Development)	52	61.17
Industrial Relations	60	70.58
Wages	40	47.05
Social Security	40	47.05
Productivity	38	44.70
Family Planning	38	44.70
Labour Economics	23	27.05
Civics	25	29.41
I.L.O.	28	32.94
Co-operatives	30	35.29

The perception of workers on sophisticated objectives of the Workers' Education Programme and their relation to their context would obviously be at a low profile. Since majority of them were interested in the growing living standards and the immediate returns, they get from the activities they perform. Unless the Programme is linked up with their career, it is unrealistic to assume any control or regulation over realising the objectives of the Programme.

A good number of topics taught to them deal with their rights and privileges, trade unionism and other topics of individual interest. But the emphasis on productivity, social security, family planning, education etc., was very low when compared to with earlier topics. This was evident from Table 5.19.

The following Table 5.26 delineates the workers' interests towards different subjects and indicates that interests towards the major fields. Only 49 have responded to the question.

Table—5.26

Workers' interest towards different subjects in ULC

Subjects	*Number*	*Percentage*
Trade unions	42	85.71
Labour laws	42	85.71
Productivity	17	34.69
Industrial Relations	41	83.67
Social Security	9	18.37
Family Budget	18	36.73
Health and Hygiene	17	34.69
Family Planning	18	36.73
Citizenship	31	63.26
Education	16	32.65

Teaching methods preferred. The popular method of teaching procedure being preferred was 'Discussion' method (65.88%) followed by 'Lectures' and with 'Audio-visual Aids' (62.35% each) followed by 'Debates (61.17%) and 'Seminars' (55.29%) as shown in Table 5.27.

Table—5.27

Teaching methods preferred by number of Worker Teachers

Descriptions	*Number*	*Percentage*
Lectures	53	62.35
Debates	52	61.17
Discussions	56	65.88
Role Play	55	64.70
Seminars	47	55.29
Audio-visual Aids	53	62.35

Thus, all the methods were found to be quite useful with slight variations and it can also be understood that the discussion method was the most preferred in the teaching procedures. The participation of workers in the discussion, as expressed by Worker Teachers in their personal interviews enhanced the personnel development and leadership qualities in the worker learners.

Teaching Aids. However, the teaching aids available with Worker Teachers and their use by them was not upto the mark (Table 5.28). The use of Black Board and Wall Displays were the most conventional aids (49.41 and 55.29%) while the rest of the aids were being used only by a few Worker Teachers (Table 5.28).

Table—5.28

Usage of Teaching-Aids by Worker Teachers

Teaching Aids	*Number*	*Percentage*
Black Board	42	49.41
Wall Displays	47	55.29
Radio and Records	31	36.47
Cinemas and Roleplay	28	32.94
Games and Sports	1	1.17

As was evident from the Table 5.29 below, in party to the Programme from the managements was little lesser than the expectation of the Worker Teachers and probably resulting in the discouragement of both Worker Teachers and Unit Level Class participants.

Table—5.29

Facilities and material available to Worker Teachers to conduct Unit Level Classes

Facility	*Availability*			
	Yes		*No*	
	n	%	*N*	%
Teaching Material	41	48.23	44	51.76
Reading Material	35	41.14	50	58.83
Study Tour	46	54.11	39	45 89
Time off Facility	47	55.30	38	44 70
Leaves/Salary Advance by Management	47	55.30	38	44.70
Other Incentives from Management	44	51.76	41	48.24

Class Room Conditions. With regard to the conditions of class room, only 10% of the Worker Teachers were satisfied with class room conditions while more than 67% of them were not satisfied and considered the class room conditions as poor. A majority of them have expressed that the trade unions should take initiation to provide these conditions (Table 5.30).

Table—5.30

Quality of facilities in the class room as expressed by Worker Teachers

	Worker Teachers					
	Good		*Average*		*Poor*	
	f	%	*f*	%	*f*	%
Lighting	16	18.82	23	27.06	46	54.12
Seating	16	18.82	17	20.00	52	61.18
Cleanliness	–	–	19	22.35	66	77.65
Library	8	9.41	30	35.30	47	55.29
Refreshments	6	7.06	16	18.82	63	74.12
Supervision	3	3.53	11	12.94	71	83.53
Provision for Teaching aids	11	12.94	16	18.82	58	68.24
Overall percentage	**60**	**10.08**	**132**	**22.19**	**403**	**67.73**

The personal observations of the investigator were as follows. The three of the four private sector undertakings do not have proper class rooms and in all the industries, provision for handling more number of classes was very far from near adequacy when compared to the number of Worker Teachers in the industry, thus contributing to enhance the number of inactive Worker Teachers .

Enrolment and Involvement. The enrolment of workers into the Unit Level Classes has been a difficult task in all the industries as was expressed by the Worker Teachers conducting Unit Level Classes. Only 20% of workers have joined the Unit Level Classes on their own while another 25% were joined under the influence of the concerned trade union and managements. Nearly 55% were mobilised or motivated by the Worker Teachers or their colleagues (Table 5.31).

Table—5.31

Motivation versus enrolment of workers into Unit Level Classes

Motivation	*Number joined*	*Percentage*
Voluntarily (Self)	20	20.41
Motivation by Trade Unions	16	24.49
Motivation by Management	8	
Motivation by Worker Teachers	34	55.00
Motivation by colleagues	20	

As can be seen from Table 5.32, the involvement of participants in different aspects of their class room work has not exceeded 28% and this indirectly indicates, (i) the ability of Worker Teachers to motivate the learners and/or (ii) the poor response from the workers towards the programme. Of these indications, the latter seems to be more probably as most of the workers have joined not on their own, but on the influence of the others (Table 5.31).

Table 5.32

Involvement of participants in the Unit Level Classes

Type of Activity	*Active persons*	
	Number	*Percentage*
Preparing Notes	16	18.82
Participating in Discussion	19	22.36
Reading relevant Literature	23	27.06
Simply listening	16	18.82
Question-Answer	11	12.94

Co-operation from Authorities. Nearly 15% of the Worker Teachers felt that the co-operation they receive from management was poor and another 28% consider the support was not sufficient (Table 5.33).

Table—5.33

Degree of Co-operation received from managements and C.B.W.E. in conducting the programme

Authority	*Degree of co-operation*							
	Very Good		*Good*		*Fair*		*Poor*	
	n	%	*n*	%	*n*	%	*n*	%
Management	8	9.41	41	48.23	24	28.23	12	14.11
C.B.W.E.	11	12.94	38	44.70	22	25.88	14	16.47

However, 9.41% of the Worker Teachers expressed that the support they receive from their management is very good and most of them belong to public sector undertakings. 48.23% of the Worker Teachers have considered the management co-operation as just good. A similar opinion trend of the Worker Teachers on the co-operation they received from C.B.W.E., is recorded in the Table 5.33.

The co-operation of the management in providing various facilities for conducting the Unit Level Classes is shown in Table 5.29.

Availability of Reading Material. Apart from the topics taught in the Unit Level Classes, the availability of reading material influenced greatly in motivating the workers to learn in a better way. However, most of the industries and trade unions are not supplying adequate reading material and the funds available for the programme were very meagre to produce reading material for the use of learners. Among other factors that influenced, proper learning by the workers included, lack of personnel for guiding the learners and want of reading room were the most prominent reasons (Table 5.34).

Table—5.34

Problems for study as expressed by workers

Reasons	*Number*	*Percentage*
Scarcity of Reading Material	52	53.06
Want of Reading Room	30	30.61
Lack of personnel guiding the learners	16	16.33

Efficiency of Worker Teachers. Several workers have also emphasized the role of Worker Teachers as factors influencing their interest in the programme. Nearly 1/3rd of the respondents were not perfectly satisfied with the way of their Worker Teachers , conducting the Unit Level Classes (Table 5.35). it is interesting to note that 86% of the group of workers belonged to urban community and mostly hailed from Forward Castes.

Table—5.35

Degree of satisfaction felt by workers

Satisfaction with the conduct of ULC by Worker Teachers	*Number*	*Percentage*
Very good	16	16.33
Well	16	16.33
Satisfactory	34	34.69
To some extent	28	28.57
Not proper or not upto the mark	4	4.08

Cognition attitude. On the question of attitude of management, union, supervisory staff and colleagues, as was perceived by the workers delineated in Table 5.36. The overall attitude of the people surrounding them at their work place can be summarised as 22.45% as very good, 47.45% as fair and 30.10% as poor.

Table—5.36

Cognition attitude by different groups as expressed by workers

	Worker Teachers					
Facility	*Very Good*		*Fair*		*Poor*	
	n	*%*	*n*	*%*	*n*	*%*
Management	18	18.37	44	44.90	36	36.73
Union	32	32.65	38	38.78	28	28.57
Supervisors	22	22.45	44	44.90	32	32.65
Colleagues	16	16.33	60	61.22	22	22.45

Personal satisfaction. Based on the following information in Table 5.37, the personal satisfaction of the Worker Teachers is analysed. Only 57.65% of the Worker Teachers were satisfied with the programme, and the others have expressed various reasons like co-operation received from management, co-operation of participants, facilities in the class room etc.

Table—5.37

Sense of satisfaction in Worker Teachers

Degree of satisfaction	*Number*		*Percentage*
Fully	25	49	57.65
Moderately	24		
Not unsatisfied	20	36	42.35
Unsatisfied	16		

On the satisfaction, the workers derived from the Unit Level Classes, the trend seems to be very discouraging as the workers were not satisfied with the programmes constituted more than a half of the total respondents. This degree of unsatisfaction can be comparable with that of Worker Teachers as shown in Table 5.37. On the whole, the programme yielded half satisfaction to the actual participation (Table 5.38).

Table—5.38

Satisfaction felt by workers in receiving the training

Performance	*Number*	*Percentage*
Highly satisfied	14	14.29
Moderately satisfied	6	6.12
Minimal	24	24.49
Not satisfied	54	55.10

On the functioning of the Workers' Education Programme in their respective unions, about 23.08% of the trade union representatives were not satisfied. However, the rest have satisfied in various degrees as shown in Table 5.39.

Table—5.39

Degree of satisfaction expressed by trade union leaders towards Workers' Education Programme

Degree of satisfaction	*Number*	*Percentage*
Very good	2	15.38
Good	3	23.08
Moderate	5	38.46
Poor	3	23.08

On the co-operation and assistance of the union, to the Workers' Education Programme, most of the representatives were not satisfied while the rest have graded it as from moderate to good. It is apparent from the reasons they have given, finances have been the major limiting factors (Table 5.40).

Table—5.40

Degree of satisfaction expressed by trade union leaders towards co-operation of their union

Degree of satisfaction	*Number*	*Percentage*
Very good	–	–
Good	2	15.38
Moderate	2	15.38
Poor	9	69.24

The reasons for dissatisfaction were analysed and several commonalities in them were shown in Table 5.41

Table—5.41

Reasons for dissatisfaction as expressed by trade union leaders

Reasons	*Number*	*Percentage*
Lack of facilities	4	30.77
Disinterest among workers	7	53.85
Financial constraints	9	69.24
Low key co-operation from:		
(i) Management	5	38.46
(ii) C.B.W.E.	7	53.85

The reasons expressed by the trade union respondents have greater impact on the programme (Table 5.41). Of all, financial constraints and the co-operation from management and Central Board for Workers' Education were limiting the extent of co-operation from the union to the Workers' Education Programme. This situation has resulted in the increase of non-active Worker Teachers and consequently workers also.

Suggestions

Out of the 85 respondents, most of the Worker Teachers have expressed their opinions, advice and suggestions for the successful implementation of the programme:

(*a*) that first of all, there is every need of increased co-operation from the management side as well as unions and the C.B.W.E.;

(*b*) emphasized the role of managements and unions in publishing the brochures in the regional language so as to supply enough reading material;

(*c*) managements should provide Worker Teachers a special time-off to enable them to attend the classes;

(*d*) provision of accommodation for class rooms, study tours, teaching aids, supply of text books and stationary *in gratis;*

(*e*) to motivate Worker Teachers and workers by providing incentives or increments; some scholarships may be given to the workers who are keen to pursue further studies;

(*f*) modification of syllabus so as to cater the needs specific to their profession and extension of training period from three months to six-eight months;

(*g*) enhancement of honorarium to a satisfactory level;

(*h*) that the government should pass a legislation for the compulsory particiapation of each and every worker in the Workers' Education Classes and to link up with the career advancement.

A good number of the (93.88%) workers felt that the programme is to be carried out by the managements and link with the career advancement. Only 6.82% of the workers favoured the takeover by the trade unions.

A list of necessities suggested by the worker trainees was given in Table 5.42, which would be recognised as factors influencing improvements in the programme.

Table—5.42

Response of workers towards different necessities for the improvement of the programme

Necessities	*Number proposed*	*Percentage*
Management and union co-operation	46	46.94
Deputation of Resource Persons	40	40.82
Provision of time allowance	30	30.61
Organisation of Seminars	36	36.73
Publishing Reading Material	26	26.53
Supply of Audio-visual aids	18	18.37
Permanent class room and Library facility	10	10.20
Additional Bonus and Increments to the trained	34	34.69
Compulsorisation of the programme	40	40.82

Suggestions by Trade Unions. Trade union leaders were also very uncertain of the present approach of the Workers' Education Programme in realising its objectives. The respondents to the questionnaire and some others with whom exclusive interviews were conducted have offered several suggestions, which they feel, will make the Workers' Education Programme realise its objectives. The suggestions offered by the trade union leaders have been described below.

The most common suggestion was to provide increments to those who have been trained as the Worker Teachers and in Unit Level Classes.

The next suggestion in the order was that the entire cost of the programme should be borne by the C.B.W.E., and the concerned managements and release the grants well in advance to the trade unions, so that the work of Workers' Education Programme will not be hampered.

Yet, another suggestion offered by the trade unions, is related to the basic infrastructural facility for conducting the Programmes. The location of the class room; provision of space for Worker Teachers preparing for the class; transport facilities to the workers, Worker Teachers to reach their places after the class etc., are some of the hindrances which indirectly affecting the attendance, regularity and supervision of the programme. The trade unions wanted these basic facilities are to be first established and then conduct the programme.

Impact. The influence of the training was indirectly measured based on the objective number three through the ratios between income to savings and debts; frequency of absenteeism in the work, the size of the family etc.

The income range of the workers varied from industry to industry as shown in the below Table 5.43

Table—5.43

The income range and mean of income of workers in different industries

*Industry**	*Range (Rs./p.m.)*	*Mean (Rs./p.m.)*
Visakhapatnam Port Trust, Visakhapatnam	2162-3600	2790
Dock Labour Board, Visakhapatnam	2400-2800	2666
Bharat Heavy Plate & Vessels Ltd., Visakhapatnam	1400-3000	2370
Ferro Alloys Corporation, Shreeramnagar	1200-2000	1572
Nellimerla Jute Mills, Nellimerla	1200-3000	1600

* Data for Andhra Pradesh Paper Mills Ltd., Rajahmundry and Sri Ramadas Motor Transport Limited, Kakinada are not available.

The habits of savings and borrowings were considered to scale the objective No.3.1 for which the savings and debts of the workers attended the Unit Level Classes were examined. More than a half of the workers (53.10%) did not have any of savings other than the compulsory savings. A good number of them belonged to public sector and have urban background. The remaining 44.90% of the workers were having the habit of savings in different degrees as sho'vn in Table 5.44.

Table—5.44

Savings of workers trained in Unit Level Classes

Savings range (% of salary)	*Number of worker respondents*	*Percentage of the respondents*
Below 10	12	12.25
10-15	14	14.29
15-20	10	10.20
20 and above	8	8.16
No savings	54	55.10

Of the 22 workers of Unit Level Classes, only 9 have cultivated the savings habit after their training, of whom only 2 individuals expressed that the habit of savings is an effect of the training they have undergone. Though 18.36% of the workers of Unit Level Classes have developed savings habit after their training, the effective influence of the training was mere 4.08%. Thus, it can be concluded that the success in the realization of the objective 3.1 is definitely below 10%.

Nearly half of the workers of Unit Level Classes responded, have debts ranging from Rs.5,000 to Rs.10,000/- while those who have debts more than Rs.10,000/- were not having any savings.

Table—5.45

Debt ranges of workers trained in Unit Level Classes

Range of debts	*Number*	*Percentage*
Below Rs.5,000/-	22	22.45
5,000–10,000	46	46.94
10,000–20,000	24	24.49
20,000 – 50,000	6	6.12
50,000/- and above	Nil	Nil

Nearly 90% of the Unit Level Class workers responded were aware of the burden of the debts. However, for various reasons, borrowings have become unavoidable. 16.33% of the Unit Level Class workers were fallen into the debt trap owing to their ill-planning or ill-practices, as was evident from their personal confessions during the interview. Thus, it is clear that this 16.33% of the Unit Level Class workers have not been influenced by the training, or the impact of Workers' Education on these people, in this regard was negligible.

Absenteeism is the factor considered as an index to the workers' responsibility towards the organisation's productivity. Apart from all eligible leaves, the leaves on loss of pay or on medical grounds indirectly indicate the workers' interest on their duty. An analysis of these two types of leaves utilised by the Unit Level Class workers is given below (Table 5.46).

Table—5.46

Utilisation of leaves by workers trained in Unit Level Classes

Duration range	*Percentage of workers' utilised*			
	Leave on loss of pay	*Medical leave*	*Both*	*Total*
Below 1 month	28.57	12.24	4.08	44.89
1–2 months	18.37	10.20	–	28.57
2 months and above	6.12	–	–	6.12
Without loss of pay and medical leave	–	–	20.42	20.42

Nearly 79.58% of the Unit Level Class workers responded have utilised the maximum leave on different terms. This high value indicates at least a half of these Unit Level Class workers and their privileges indiscriminately. Interviews with the Unit Level Class workers indicated that most of the frequent leave mongers have other affairs ranging from petty business to benami contracts, which they relate them to the economic pressures. Thus, their priority to their duty at the industry has been secondary and probably these people need training in time management.

Of the 98 Unit Level Class workers responded, only two were unmarried. All the ULC workers were aware of the importance of the wife's education. However, 57.45% of the ULC workers were married to illiterate women and none of them have tried to make their wife a literate. However, relatively more number of ULC workers were providing education to their children. However, 30.61% of the ULC workers were not taking care of their children's education also.

The ULC workers' interest towards Family Planning also varied diversely. A matrix of the Age-groups and number of children of the ULC workers were given below (Table 5.47).

Table—5.47

Matrix of different age-groups with number of workers: Children

	Number of workers with number of children					
	Nil	*1*	*2*	*3*	*4*	*5 & above*
Below 25	2	2	–	–	–	–
25-35	4	8	18	18	10	–
35-45	–	2	2	4	12	4
45-55	–	–	–	2	2	6
Total (percentage)					**24 (24.49)**	**10 (10.20)**

The above data suggests that, in spite of various Family Planning Programmes and the education provided to the ULC workers, about 59.18% of them were having 3 or more children, which not only affect their family economy but the quality life of their children. It is an irony that 7 of the 24 fathers with 4 children had their last issue after they were trained in the Unit Level Classes.

On the whole, it can be summarised that impact of training was far from realising the objective No. 2 as considerable number of trainees were not able to plan their family economics nor improved their time planning and conscious of family planning.

The opinion of Worker Teachers on scope and relevance of the syllabi and training of ULC in realising the seven objectives of the CBWE was collected and analysed. The analysis reveals that the positive impact was not upto the mark and adequate to realise the defined objectives. Nearly 30% of the Worker Teachers opined that the realisation of the objectives would be nominal (43.41%) to moderate (29.64%) and only 5.06% expressed absolute positivity while 21.86% expressed absolute negative response (Table 5.48).

Personal interviews with the individual Worker Teachers whose response was negative to Table 5.48, revealed several reasons or lacunae in the programme influencing the achievement of the Workers' Education Programme (Table 5.50).

Table—5.48

Opinion of Worker Teachers towards the objectives of the CBWE programme

Objectives of CBWE	*Degree of realisation*			
	Absolute	*Moderate*	*Minimal*	*Nil*
(*a*) Develop Nationalism	–	25	52	8
(*b*) Enable workers to participate in the social and economic development of the country	8	30	31	16
(*c*) 1. Create awareness of their socio-economic environment	3	19	41	22
2. Guide the responsibility towards family	3	22	35	25
3. Enable to perform their duties at workplace with greater ability and amicability	3	22	41	19
4. Create awareness of rights	6	25	35	19
(*d*) Develop leadership among the rank and file	5	16	39	25
(*e*) Strengthen trade unions	5	27	31	22
(*f*) Enhance democratic process in trade unions	2	33	36	14
(*g*) Enable trade unions to take over Workers' Education	8	33	28	16
Overall n (percentage)	43 (5.06)	252 (29.64)	369 (43.41)	186 (21.86)

On the first objective, 9.41% were negative and most of them expressed that the existing regionalism and casteism in their organisation do not permit to promote nationalism and other components of the said objective.

On the second objective, 16.06% have responded negatively and majority of them expressed lack of recognition, lack of dignity of labour for reasons contributing to non-participation of workers in the socio-economic development of the country.

On the objective three, majority of them felt that the syllabus is not sufficient or relevant to realise the objectives as they lack in practical approach for creating the awareness of the socio-economic environment; other conditions like recognition, encouragement and co-operation from their superiors and subordinates have influence over the performance at their work place; and the ideologies and individual attitudes of the Worker Teachers may often misled in creating awareness of workers' rights.

The common reason that is influencing the realisation of the objectives 4, 5 and 6, as expressed by majority of Worker Teachers, the role of money, politics and casteism in the development and strengthening of trade union. The above reasons were delineated in Table 5.49.

Table—5.49

Opinions expressed by Worker Teachers towards the CBWE programme

Opinion	*Objectives**										*Overall*	
	a	*b*	*c1*	*c2*	*c3*	*c4*	*d*	*e*	*f*	*g*	*No.*	*%*
Syllabus not sufficient	–	2	14	9	3	8	–	5	–	6	47	55.29
Syllabus not relevant	–	3	–	8	3	4	3	–	3	4	28	32.94
Other reasons	8	9	6	–	13	2	17	9	11	6	81	95.29
Don't know	–	2	2	8	0	5	5	8	–	–	30	35.29
Total	**8**	**16**	**22**	**25**	**19**	**19**	**25**	**22**	**14**	**16**	**186**	–

* for objectives a-g please see Table: 5.48.

Table—5.50

Degree of negativity expressed by Worker Teachers on the objectives of programme

Causes of negativity			*Number expressed to 5.48*	*% of negative*	*% of total respondents*	*Common reason*
(a)	1.	Syllabus not sufficient	–	–	–	–
	2.	Syllabus not relevant	–	–	–	–
	3.	Other reasons*	8	–	9.41	Existing regionalism and casteism
	4.	Don't know	–	–	–	–
(b)	1.	Syllabus not sufficient	2	12.50	2.50	–
	2.	Syllabus not relevant	3	18.75	3.52	–
	3.	Other reasons	9	56.25	10.58	Lack of dignity of labour and non-encouragement lack of recognition
	4.	Don't know	2	12.50	2.35	–
(c1)	1.	Syllabus not sufficient	14	63.63	16.47	–
	2.	Syllabus not relevant	–	–	–	–
	3.	Other reasons	6	27.28	7.05	Lack of practical approach
	4.	Don't know	–	–	–	–
(c2)	1.	Syllabus not sufficient	9	36.00	10.58	–
	2.	Syllabus not relevant	8	32.00	9.41	–
	3.	Other reasons	–	–	–	–
	4.	Don't know	8	32.00	9.41	–
(c3)	1.	Syllabus not sufficient	3	15.79	3.52	–
	2.	Syllabus not relevant	3	15.79	3.52	–
	3.	Other reasons	13	68.42	15.29	Other conditions at work environment
	4.	Don't know	–	–	–	–

(Contd...)

1			2	3	4	5
(c4)	1.	Syllabus not sufficient	8	42.10	9.41	–
	2.	Syllabus not relevant	4	21.05	4.70	–
	3.	Other reasons	2	10.52	2.35	Often can be mobilised by WTs
	4.	Don't know	5	26.33	5.88	–
(d)	1.	Syllabus not sufficient	–	–	–	–
	2.	Syllabus not relevant	3	12.00	3.52	–
	3.	Other reasons	17	68.00	20.00	Leadership is governed by money, politics and caste
	4.	Don't know	5	20.00	5.88	–
(e)	1.	Syllabus not sufficient	5	22.72	5.88	–
	2.	Syllabus not relevant	–	–	–	–
	3.	Other reasons	9	40.90	10.58	Leadership is governed by money, politics and caste
	4.	Don't know	–	–	–	–
(f)	1.	Syllabus not sufficient	8	36.38	9.41	–
	2.	Syllabus not relevant	3	21.42	3.52	–
	3.	Other reasons	11	78.58	12.94	Leadership is governed by money, politics and caste
	4.	Don't know	–	–	–	–
(g)	1.	Syllabus not sufficient	6	37.50	7.05	–
	2.	Syllabus not relevant	4	25.00	4.70	–
	3.	Other reasons	6	37.50	7.05	Varying perception of WTs
	4.	Don't know	–	–	–	–

During the personal interviews with the trade union respondents, almost all have expressed confidence in the beneficial effects of the Workers' Education Programme. However, on individual objectives, the response varied widely (Table 5.51). On the whole, only 18.80% of the trade union respondents were perfectly positive on the realisation of the Workers' Education Programme's objectives while 23.08% were perfectly negative on the subject.

Table—5.51

Opinion of Trade Union Leaders towards the objectives of the CBWE programme

Objectives of CBWE	*Degree of realisation*			
	Absolute	*Moderate*	*Minimal*	*Nil*
(a) Develop Nationalism	1	4	8	–
(b) Enable workers to participate in the social and economic development of the country	2	6	1	4
(c) 1. Create awareness of their socio-economic environment	–	1	5	7
2. Guide the responsibility towards family	1	3	5	4
3. Enable to perform their duties at workplace with greater ability and amicability	3	5	4	1
4. Create awareness of rights	4	7	2	–
(d) Develop leadership among the rank and file	4	2	4	3
(e) Strengthen trade unions	4	5	3	1
(f) Enhance democratic process in trade unions	7	5	1	–
(g) Enable trade unions to takeover Workers' Education	–	1	5	7
Overall n (percentage)	**26 (20.00)**	**39 (30.00)**	**38 (29.20)**	**27 (20.80)**

Table 5.51 delineates the views of trade union respondents in the realisation of individual objectives of the Workers' Education Programme. It is of interest to record that 54% of the trade union

respondents have expressed that under the present conditions, the final objective of the Workers' Education Programme cannot be realised as trade unions will not be able to takeover the Workers' Education Programme for the reasons mentioned in the Table 5.41.

On the whole, realisation of the objectives of the CBWE as can be seen from the cumulative opinion of both the Trade Union Leaders and Worker Teachers (Table 5.52) nearly 63.26% of the members were not confident of the programme's approach.

Table—5.52

Cumulative opinion of the Trade Union Leaders and Worker Teachers on the realisation of the objectives of the CBWE programme

	Degree of realisation			
Objectives of CBWE	*Absolute*	*Moderate*	*Minimal*	*Nil*
(a) Develop Nationalism	1	29	60	8
(b) Enable workers to participate in the social and economic development of the country	10	36	32	20
(c) 1. Create awareness of their socio-economic environment	3	20	46	29
2. Guide the responsibility towards family	4	25	40	29
3. Enable to perform their duties at workplace with greater ability and amicability	6	27	45	20
4. Create awareness of rights	10	32	37	19
(d) Develop leadership among the rank and file	9	18	43	28
(e) Strengthen trade unions	9	38	37	14
(f) Enhance democratic process in trade unions	9	32	34	23
(g) Enable trade unions to take over Workers' Education	8	34	33	23
Overall n (percentage)	**69 (7.05)**	**291 (29.69)**	**407 (41.53)**	**213 (21.73)**

The incidence of taking disciplinary action against workers has fallen greatly during the last 10 years, in all the industries with a single exception of the NJM. The number of mandays lost also decreased steeply. However, the managements while answering a question expressed that a majority of the workers were not serious of maintaining promptness and punctuality. The management expressed that the average work realised from each worker was much lesser than the amount expected from them. This is more pronounced in the public sector industries.

Among the private sector, NJM had a very bad situation of industrial relations and was under lock-out for more than a year during the last 5 years because of severe labour problems. of the other three private sector industries, the per capita turn over was relatively low at FACOR, which can be compared with that of the public sector industries like VPT and DLB.

The personal observations of the author revealed that serious wastage of time is taking place in all the industries, in general and in public sector in particular. A good number of people waste their time during their working hours, by involving themselves in conversations and avoidable activities. Significantly, good number of workers would not be at respective places during their working hours and will go on friendly visits to other sections. The number of mandays lost indirectly indicates the relative change in the aptitude of workers and their commitment to the industry.

Since the implementation of the programme, the percentage of the total workforce covered indicates that the coverage was considerably good in VPT among public sector industries and in FACOR and NJM among private sector industries. However, the ratio of Worker Teachers to Workers learners was very high in NJM (286W/WT) which indicates the intensive activity of the Worker Teachers when compared with those at the other industries. This intensive activity of Worker Teachers is mainly because of the interest of the Worker Teachers supported by the encouragement and co-operation given by the respective trade unions.

6
DISCUSSION

With the rapid technological changes everywhere, and with the increasing momentum of industrialisation in most of the under-developed countries, both management and labour have been faced with wider responsibilities and new problems. A primary factor in the development of constructive labour management relations is the attitude of management and that of labour. To a very large extent, these attitudes are formed by education and experience and modified by the current pressures of the industrial and social situation in each country. This has placed an accent on adaptation and learning, and has given considerable impetus to management development and Workers' Education, particularly in the industrially less advanced countries, where the needs are greatest and the problems are acute.

Over large areas of the world, trade unions are young and inexperienced. They often need to find a genuine leadership from among workers themselves, to build up a strong and stable trade union membership and to educate the members in the process of collective negotiation and in the ways of union organisation and activities. The ILO has been conscious of these needs and built up its service in the field of Workers' Education by launching the Workers' Education Programme in 1956.[1]

During the same period, based on the observations of the Royal Commission of Labour, 1931 which viewed that the root cause of all industrial unrests was the then prevalent illiteracy among the industrial workers, the Indian Workers' Education Programme has evolved. But, the Indian situation warranted to drive illiteracy first and then the task of educating the workers of their requirements that change from time to time. The basic objectives of Workers' Education in India and that of ILO are more or less similar.

This greater overlap between the objectives of the Workers' Education of the CBWE and ILO, provides substantial evidence to describe the influence of ILO on the Workers' Education Programme in India. As described earlier, ILO and the CBWE envisage strong trade unions with an educated workforce who could fairly carry on their functional and civic responsibilities and contribute to the socio-economic development.

However, for ILO, Workers' Education is a continuing process, but in India, the programme generally ends with the completion of training. Very few have the chance of participating in the refresher courses, while the scope for advanced studies is totally absent. On the other hand, the ILO strongly advocates continuing education for the workers with special reference to the change in their requirements from time to time.

The syllabi of the Indian Workers' Education Programme, though formulated to address the seven objectives of the programme defined by CBWE, it can be compared with the contents of the syllabi suggested by an ILO expert, Manuel Dia, for Asian Region.[2] However, the hierarchical exposure of worker learners to the programme suggested by Manuel Dia, such as gradual exposure from basic courses to specialised and advanced courses is absent in the Indian Programme. The course content in the Indian Programme remained more or less unchanged for the past several years and the dearth of scope, to deal with technical or vocational education, has been very distinct. Further, irrespective of the type of industry and the basic educational level, the workers have to study the same syllabi and undergo the same training.

Unlike the Indian Programme, the ILO Programmes regularly change based upon the needs identified by the organisation. During the past two decades, a dramatic change has been taken place in the Workers' Education Programmes sponsored by ILO. An in-depth review of the Workers' Education Programmes was undertaken by the ILO Governing Body at its 188th session in 1972 and 189th session in 1973 identified priority areas which included the economic education, the development of educational programmes, co-operatives, environmental questions etc.[3]

Such a dynamic change has not taken place in the programmes of Workers' Education in India. The course content, and the approach adopted for training have not been revised or modified with the changing times or situations.

As described in Chapter II, the objectives of Workers' Education Programme in India, have consisted of seven points. The twelve components of Workers' Education syllabi fairly covers all the seven objectives of the Programme, as per the following Table 6.1.

Table—6.1

Table showing the coverage of topics under various components of the Worker Teacher's syllabus with special reference to the objectives of the Worker's Education Programme

Objectives of CBWE		*Components (Topics) of Syllabus*
(a)		All topics under II
(b)		II (4); III (1); All topics of IV; IX (1, 3, 4) and X (2).
(c)	1.	All topics of VII
	2.	X (1, 4, 5)
	3.	VI (11, 13)
	4.	I (7); VII (1); XI (1, 2, 3)
(d)		VI (9)
(e)		VI (1, 4, 5, 6, 10)
(f)		I (9); VI (12)
(g)		All topics of XII

For the code of references under objectives of C.B.W.E., please refer Table 5.52.

For the code of references under components of the syllabus please refer Appendix-III.

Though the topics were very relevant, but they were beyond the reception capacity of the workers. Further, these subjects have to be taught by the people who has just 3 months training in teaching and were having a low basic education. A distinct difference between the age and educational qualifications of Worker Teachers and worker trainees may be essential to maintain the pious relationship between the two. Both the Worker Teachers and worker trainees mostly belonged to 26-45 age groups. On the other hand, the general education level of both the Worker Teachers and workers was more or less equal, so also their nature of jobs. Majority of both the communities belonged to technical types of job.

As was evident from Tables 5.25 and 5.26, the topics preferred by both the Worker Teachers and worker trainees deal only with their rights and privileges rather than the duties and responsibilities, perhaps the wide syllabi with a short course duration must have played a limiting role in restricting the interests of the worker trainees.

Thus, the approach and sequence in teaching the subject is also not found to be satisfactory as was evident from the present study and also as was evident from the sequence in the syllabi. For instance, the Economics component in the worker teacher syllabi deal mainly with wages, bonus and allowances with special reference to the productivity of the industry, cost of living and comparative per capita incomes of different regions. Compared to this, the scheme of ILO has a more logical and realistic way of developing the subject. For instance, teaching of "Economics" in the ILO scheme can be taken as the best example. The ILO scheme starts with a consideration of the workers' standard of living and then moves on to the relationship between workers and enterprises, before discussing the national and international frame work within which workers and employers earn their living.[4] Thus, it is believed that the first step in introducing workers to the subject of Economics must be to prove that it is of direct relevance to their working lives, and one which as trade unionists, they would do well to investigate.

Some of the vital topics like collective bargaining, co-operatives, occupational health and safety etc., which were highlighted by the ILO, appear not to have received due importance in the syllabi of Indian Workers' Education

Programme, since these topics appear at a sub-component level. Similarly, the emphasis on leadership development also is not as adequate as required by the objectives of the Programme. Considering the low level of basic education of the workers in general, the syllabi for Workers' Education seems to be very complex. This complex syllabi, with a short course duration and minimal facilities, perhaps affected the quality of education provided to the workers. This might have contributed to the growing disinterest among the Worker Teachers and worker trainees.

On the other hand, the Programme offered wide scope for some of the Worker Teachers who have vested interests and utilised the Programme as a tool to promote their personal interests. Often the innocent worker trainees are carried away by the ideologies and views of such Worker Teachers resulting in the loss of uniformity and increased anomalies in understanding of the subject.

In the present study, those Worker Teachers who wish to become trade union leaders, gain popular support among their worker trainees by simply over emphasizing the rights rather than the responsibilities. A good number of Worker Teachers have held some influential posts in the respective trade unions, while none of the worker trainees could come to the level of becoming a trade union leader. Kakkar[5] also made a similar observation, and opined that the Worker Teachers are generally leaders of their union and they do not leave any opportunity for others to become leaders. He further says that if any rank and file is holding any key position in the trade union, it is not because of the Workers' Education but because of his personal contacts. The Workers' Education is being taken as a tool to develop these personal contacts. Thus, Kakkar[5] states that the Workers' Education classes are serving as a stage for the trade union propaganda which, as he observes, forfeits the aim of the scheme.

Mahar[6] opined that Workers' Education has succeeded in creating trade union consciousness amongst Worker Teachers and worker trainees, while Gandhi[7] considered the Programme a limited success which she related to various social, economic, political and general educational issues.

As was evident from Table 5.18, majority of the Worker Teachers who joined the Programme have improved social relations. Incidentally, most of these Worker Teachers are the persons who held different posts in their union executive. Similarly, their involvement in politics is also considerable and only 18.83% of the Worker Teachers are not interested in politics. Some of the Worker Teachers have obtained membership and responsibilities in some special committees constituted by the concerned industry/ unions. These appointments have enhanced the status of the appointed personnel. A good number of Worker Teachers are in such posts and most of them are active Worker Teachers . Such type of participation by worker trainees was meagre and negligible.

Thus, it is clear that Workers' Education Programme has succeeded in developing leadership at least among Worker Teachers . This fact reflects also from the compositions of the trade union executives. In the earlier days, these unions were used to be led by outsiders, while in the recent times, almost all the unions of the seven industries were led by the respective worker leaders. A good number of them are trained as Worker Teachers .

Most of the objectives of Workers' Education Programme are dependent upon effective training and the quality of the education received by the workers. To ensure this quality of education, ILO recommends the use of audio-visual aids, seminaries and other pedagogical methods. For this purpose ILO has developed enormous material like manuals of Workers' Education, Journal of Labour Education etc.

ILO provides film strips and other audio-visual aids on different subjects. However, those aids are not suitable to the Visakhapatnam region where 'Telugu' is the regional language. It is highly essential that the CBWE is to take further lead in developing the audio-visual aids in different regional languages, so as to equip the Worker Teachers for effective teaching. In the Indian situation, the majority of the workforce are with school qualifications and the contents of the syllabi is too long to be taught effectively in three months. To overcome this, at least to some extent, use of audio-visual aids is highly essential. Though the audio-visual aids are being used, the available packages are not adequate to cover most of the vital components in the syllabi. Unlike ILO, the CBWE is not successful in the dissemination of information and knowledge as was evident from the reflections of Worker Teachers and worker trainees with regard to study material available to them. Similarly, the emphasis on refresher courses, or not organising seminars and conferences was very poor. Audio-visual aids, besides educating the workers in a more effective way, attract many, especially in a country like India where cinema is known to be the best media of reaching the masses.

The overall objective is to equip the labour to help themselves to participate in the socio-economic development and this has to be achieved through education. Active realisation of the objectives of the Workers' Education Programme can be indicated by healthy mental attitude of workers to work-discipline, productivity, leadership and a better participation in the socio-economic development.

As discussed earlier, the Programme succeeded in promoting leadership qualities among some of the workers. However, the attitudes of leaders towards work-discipline is much controversial as some of them, expressed by the management representatives in their study, they were more conscious of their rights and privileges than the duties and responsibilities. Further, the attitude of some of the Worker Teachers as also observed by Kakkar,[5] would always try to impress upon the workers about the role played by their unions or certain individuals in getting more facilities for them and also flout other unions resulting in the increase of tensions in the industry because of inter-union rivalries. Thus, the competition among the trade unions has resulted in the over protection of the workers and thereby most of the managements are afraid of growing indiscipline.

The attitude towards work-discipline can be indirectly gauged by several parameters like time keeping and punctuality, conflicts at the work place, wastage of time at work etc. The incidence of disciplinary action against workers declined steeply over the past 10 years. However, this decline is perhaps due to the increased resistance of trade unions as attributed by the managements.

In the earlier days, the managements had full control over their workers and this authority was misused to exploit the workers with less regard. However, during this period, the sincerity, punctuality and loyalty of the workers were said to be rarely in doubt. After the emergence of trade unions, most of the actions of the managements have come under scrutiny and the managements needed the co-operation of trade unions to exercise their control over workers. Wherever, the trade union leaders are biased and showed vested interests, the managements of such industries have minimal control over taking disciplinary action against the indiscipline, even in genuine cases. This has resulted in the undue over-confidence among the workers and eroded the ethics of work. However, this is not the case in all the industries.

As per the versions of some senior workers, this attitude of negligence of time is growing for the past 15 years. Barring the NJM, which was in lock-out, among the other industries, workers in DLB and FACOR appear to be relatively less conscious of time factor. One of the representatives from the managements opined that "though negligence of time is a serious crime in terms of productivity, but is presently considered as a petty matter against which no action can be taken". Personal observations of the author also revealed attitude of growing negligence of time factor. Besides punctuality, wastage of time is another factor to guage the quality of work discipline. Personal observations and experiences revealed that serious wastage of time is taking place in all the industries. This is also evident from the management's views of the reduced per capita productivity of the workers. Thus, the impact of the Programme is promoting work discipline is not so significant as was also confirmed by the cumulative opinion of the trade unions and workers teachers (Please see (iii) of Table 5.52).

Therefore, it is most likely that the effect of Workers' Education Scheme on the mental attitude of the workers to the work discipline and productivity is marginal. Without these, the workers' participation in socio-economic development is not possible. Perhaps the failures of Workers' Education Scheme in this regard may be due to unbalanced syllabi and absence of continuing education for workers as advised by ILO.

On the need for Workers' Education, all sects in the society as well as in the industry have unanimously felt that the programme is essential. However, in the present study, the management representatives in the public sector are of view that the scheme has failed in properly educating the workers as the people who run the programme emphasized the part of rights and ignored the part of duties. The co-operation received by the Worker Teachers from their respective managements was not satisfactory as can be seen from Table 5.33. It is apparent from Table 5.29, that the facilities and teaching material provided for the Worker Teachers was not upto the mark. Only a half of the Worker Teachers or less than that were receiving these from their managements or unions. Only 10% of the Worker Teachers were satisfied with the class-room conditions, which were far from adequate in accommodation, facilities and other respects, to create a congenial atmosphere to train workers before or after their working hours. All these indicate that the managements were playing a role obligatorily but not with the actual spirit of the Programme to have better industrial relations. This may be due to several factors like inability to provide optimal class-room and library facilities to all the trade unions existing in their industry; loss of control over the workers due to increased resistance from trade unions and misuse of the Programme by some leaders for their vested interests. Thus, it is highly essential to develop work ethics, through democratic processes within and outside the unions.

Kakkar[5] opined that the Indian trade union had adopted a rather passive role in undertaking Workers' Education because of the inadequate finances and weak organisation. Thus, the need for Government sponsoring of the Workers' Education Programme became essential. The Government of India began to sponsor Workers' Education Programme through the CBWE established specially for this purpose and with a network of 49 regional and 9 Sub-Regional centres, covering the entire nation.

The number of Worker Teachers trained in the scheme, since its inception, and similarly the number of workers trained in the programme are very meagre when compared to the size of the country's work force. The situation is the same, even at the micro-level, say in each industry. The number of Worker Teachers trained and the number of worker trainees are small fractions when compared to the size of the work force (Please see Table 4.1). The scenario of the private sector is much worse.

If the numbers of Worker Teachers and worker trainees produced per annum for the past 10 years are taken into account, we find a declining trend indicating that the pace of educating the workers can never match the pace of the growing work force. Thus, even if the scheme is run for several more decades, the objectives of having educated work force cannot be realised. Here, in the term 'Educated Work Force' education is not referred to general education in the mainstream, but, refers to that education which realised the seven objectives of the Workers' Education Scheme in India, as described by the Central Board for Workers' Education.

On the realisation of the objectives of CBWE through the Workers' Education Scheme, the workers in the present study were optimistic of the results. Even the trade unions appear to be not so keen on implementing the programme, mainly because of meagre financial resources, lack of efficient personnel and ignorance of unexposed workers and Worker Teachers. The ratio between the Worker Teachers and worker trainees increased gradually, over the past 10 years, which is the positive sign for the development of the programme. However, the irregularity in attending the ULCs and the frequency of the conduct of ULC s indicate that the initial zeal of being trained is not maintained throughout the training as was also confessed in the personal interviews with the workers. This fact was reflected in the opinions on the satisfaction they obtained from being trained.

All these have resulted in the increase of inactive Worker Teachers and thereby increasing irregularity among worker trainees in attending the ULCs. Further, these factors have resulted in the decrease of enrolment during the successive years. Perhaps, because of these reasons the number of trained Worker Teachers and worker trainees have sharply fallen over the past 10 years in spite of the increased funding and a better network.

Most of the Worker Teachers and trainees have not showed good interest towards the survey and it has been difficult to make them even accept the questionnaire. Of the work teachers trained in all the industries, only 80.16% have accepted the questionnaire; only 5.58% worker trainees and 61.90% trade union representatives have accepted the questionnaire.

Even the recovery of the questionnaire, has become a difficult task. Only 3.40% of the Worker Teachers and none of the worker trainees have returned without being reminded of the duly filled-in questionnaires. The rest needed greater efforts to motivate them for answering the questionnaire. 37.86% of the Worker Teachers questioned or 91.76% of the total responded Worker Teachers have need extra motivation; and 18.15% of the worker trainees questioned or all the total responded worker trainees, needed motivation of greater degree to make them involved in the survey. This may also suggest that greater motivation of the workers, may help in the better involvement of the workers in the Workers' Education Programme.

As per Table 5.19, most of the workers have joined the scheme to know their rights and duties; labour acts, and their welfare schemes but unfortunately not so keen on understanding industrial relations, productivity or safety.

Inactivity of Worker Teachers is yet another problem. Because of the inter-union rivalries and weak unions, most of the Worker Teachers were not able to provide facilities comparable to those provided by the stronger unions of the same industry. Hence, the Worker Teachers of the weaker unions, mostly tend to become inactive. Many of the inactive Worker Teachers belonged to weaker unions in the present study. Comparatively, absenteeism of worker trainees to the ULCs was greater than the inactivity of Worker Teachers .

Though the reasons expressed by the workers (Pl. see Table 5.23), influenced to a greater extent for their irregularity, other factors that have a bearing on the frequency of the ULC batches conducted per annum by individual Worker Teachers , indirectly indicates, as was also expressed by the Worker Teachers in the personal interviews with them, that most of the workers enrolled for ULCs did not continue because of the better facilities being provided by their fellow Worker Teachers because of their being in a stronger union or because of their influential position within the union etc. On the other hand, unsuitable timings in the conduct of ULCs has been another major factor of irregularity in the worker trainees. All these may have greatly effected the quality of teaching and enthusiasm of Worker Teachers.

Only 20% of the workers have joined on their own. This was the group of worker trainees, who have joined with interest. Others were made to join with the motivation of some or other people. It appears that, the later group was not actively participating in the ULC as some 20% of the workers only were actively involved themselves in various aspects of class activities as can be seen from Table 5.32.

This indicated that mere enrolment is not the end for motivating the workers to join the programme. The motivation should continue till the worker trainee gets actual interest in the programme so that he himself will involve in the process of learning. But it is the duty of Worker Teachers to inculcate interest among their worker trainees. However, very few worker teachers have these capabilities as majority of them were not having experience in teaching, or as described earlier, the difference in the levels of general education between the Worker Teachers and worker trainees was minimal to have command over their subjects. Thus, it is essential that the selection of Worker Teachers should be based upon certain qualifications like education, experience, attitude for teaching etc.

Therefore, it is recommended that worker teacher should have the following qualifications:

1. Should have strong attitude for learning and teaching.
2. Educational qualifications should be greater than at least 60% of the work force.
3. Should have an experience of at least 10 years of service and
4. Above 35 years of age.

People with these qualifications will be fewer in number in majority of the unions and industries. Thus, to utilise these personnel, the programme should have provisions to attract these personnel and offer them with due recognition; special allowance of time; reasonable honorarium etc. Most of the Worker Teachers were unhappy with the honorarium they receive, which appears to be not proportional to their service. The trade unions and the management should jointly take up the responsibility of identifying the Worker Teachers and to sponsor them for training. Better teaching can enhance the plight of the programme. Thus, the scope for improving the state of Workers' Education will be very wide, if the Worker Teachers are given greater encouragement.

Data in Table 5.33 delineates the degree of co-operation from the CBWE to the Worker Teachers . The CBWE should provide more reading material for the exclusive use of Worker Teachers and worker trainees. Further, the financial assistance provided by the CBWE to the trade unions was very meagre and the grants-in-aid for the programme of the CBWE provided to the trade union organisations was Rs.1.76 Crores[8] to train 6,24,349 workers of 1,304 unions. This amounts to individual trade unions will range from a low of Rs.9.47 per worker trainee to a high of Rs.69.46 per worker trainee, with a mean of Rs.29.85[8] for all unions and organisations, put together. Even the highest amount in the above range is very meagre if considered with the current growing prices, for organising a 3-month programme of the ULCs. With all these problems, the implementation part of the Workers' Education Programme was greatly affected and did not yield the desired results. The 6,24,349 workers trained in 40 years were much less in number than the work force that will be recruited every year all over India.

To enable the trade unions to take over the Workers' Education and cover maximum workers in a time-bound programme, the following suggestions are offered:

(i) Proper legislations should be made to make the Workers' Education compulsory during the first year of service in any industry and senior Worker Teachers (based on their qualifications prescribed) are to be employed exclusively for the purpose, who will be continuously organising the programme for the untrained workers.

(ii) The managements should link the programme with the career advancement of the workers and provide at least

one additional increment to those who have successfully undergone the training.

(iii) It is also desirable to have at least an objective type test at the completion of each ULC batch.

(iv) The trade unions should co-ordinate with the managements to develop work – discipline through Workers' Education and thereby contribute to the better industrial relations and healthy productivity.

(v) The course duration is to be extended from 3 months to 6 months with suitable revisions in the syllabi, emphasizing work discipline, collective bargaining, co-operatives, environment, occupational health and safety etc.

(vi) The CBWE and the managements should co-operate in developing high use of audio-visual aids for effective teaching and also improve the class-room conditions.

(vii) Involvement of Universities and Institutions dealing with Labour Education is a must for better orientation.

Sarma[9], in his study on the aspects of labour welfare and Social Security emphasized that Workers' Education is essential for a new orientation in trade union training and strategy, and to make the work force aware of their rights and responsibilities. Thirty years ago, in 1973 Kakkar[5] remarked that "Workers' Education is not having a Midas touch. The statement holds good even to date. This is beyond any doubt that Workers' Education can do miracles if properly implemented and properly understood by the managements, trade unions and the individuals in particular.

REFERENCES

1. *The ILO in a Changing World*, Report of the Director General, ILO, Geneva, 1958, pp.30-34.
2. *The Construction of Syllabi, Labour Education*, ILO, Geneva, 1983/3, p.39.
3. *Activities of the ILO*, 1972, ILO, Geneva, 1973, pp.23-24.
4. *Economics, Labour Education*, ILO, Geneva, 1983/3, p.44.
5. Kakkar, N.K., *Workers Education*, Sterling Publishers (Pvt.) Ltd., New Delhi, 1973, pp.228-239.

6. Mahar Allah, *A Critical Study of the Worker's Education Scheme in India with Special Reference to their Role in Government of India, Presses*, Doctoral Thesis, Aligarh Muslim University, Aligarh, 1979.

7. Gandhi Kalyani, *The Workers' Education Scheme of India*, Doctoral Thesis, The State University of New Jersey, USA, 1979.

8. *Review of Board's Activities, Workers' Education*, CBWE, June 1992, pp.79-94.

9. Sarma, A.M., *Aspects of Labour Welfare and Social Security*, Himalaya Publishing House, Bombay, 1981, pp.122-124.

PART—III

7

SUMMARY AND CONCLUSIONS

Trade Unions are now the biggest mass organisations, the spirit of which has gripped the minds of all sectors of people. They play an important role in good industrial relations by co-ordinating the managements and workers. The reasons for deteriorating industrial relations were identified as illiteracy, ignorance and innocence of the majority of the Indian workers. consequently, the Worker's Education Programme was launched in 1958 in India, through as Quasi Government Organisation called CBWE.

The Board functions to realise its seven well defined objectives of which the first one is concerned with the development of nationalism. The next three points emphasized the socio-economic development of the workers, and of their rights and duties at work places and in the social environment. The last four points are aimed at the development of leadership, strengthening the trade unions and enabling the trade unions to take over the responsibility of Workers' Education.

The objectives of the WEP of the CBWE have greater overlap with those of ILO, which initiated its Workers' Education activities in 1956 with the aim to "help equip the workers with the knowledge and understanding, they need not only to carryout their functional and civic responsibilities in modern society, but also to contribute fully to the whole process of economic growth and social development". This indicates the influence of ILO on formulation of the Indian programme of Workers' Education.

A brief review of the Trade Unionism revealed the need for educating the workers to make the Trade Unions stronger and self-reliant in leadership. ILO envisages strong and self-reliant Trade Unions which contribute to the socio-economic development and help themselves in improving their standards of living. The contribution of the ILO to the field of Workers' Education is delineated.

The CBWE with its 49 Regional and 9 Sub-Regional centres developed a scheme that consisted three stages of which, in the first stage post-graduates in the relevant fields will be recruited as Education Officers, for whom necessary training will be given to guide the Workers' Education Programmes.

In the second stage, selected workers of different industries sponsored by various unions will be trained as Worker Teachers to enable them to conduct training programmes to train the workers.

The trained Worker Teachers , in the third stage conduct classes for their fellow workers, at their work places and train them at the Unit Level Classes. The structure and organisation of the CBWE and the programme plan were delineated in detail.

The syllabi for training of Education Officers, Worker Teachers and Worker Trainees were formulated by the CBWE which mainly consisted components like:

> Know your country; know your industry; Productivity Education; Industrial Relations; Trade Union Movement; Labour Economics; Education for Participative Management; Public Sector Role in Economy; Population Education and Family Welfare; Labour Legislations etc.

The syllabus has been compared with that of ILO, one of an ILO expert suggested for the Asian region. Considering the levels of basic education of the Indian Workers, the syllabi formulated by CBWE and the approach adopted for the training appears to be complex and beyond the reception capacity of the learners. However, the coverage addresses all the 7 objectives of the programme.

In 1960, the CBWE has initiated a Grants-in-aid Programme for training the workers. of the total 40,60,902 workers trained since 1958-61, 6,24,349 of 1304 unions were trained under Grants-in-aid Programme.

Forty years have passed since the action programmes were implemented. However, at micro-level there was no information as to what extent the approach adopted was successful in realising the objectives of the programme. Thus, the present study was directed to:

1. evaluate and assess the effect of the Workers' Education Schemes on the development of the healthy mental attitude to work discipline, productivity, leadership and the intelligent participation of workers in social and economic development of the nation;
2. assess the degree of participation of industrial units in the Workers' Education Scheme;
3. identify the problems involved in implementing Workers' Education Scheme;
4. suggest the ways and measures to adopt at different levels–government, industry, trade union etc., to make the Workers' Education more purposeful; and
5. review the achievements of the Workers' Education Programmes.

The study was carried out at CBWE region of Visakhapatnam and in seven industries, namely, Visakhapatnam Port Trust, Dock Labour Board and Bharat Heavy Plate & Vessels Ltd., of Public Sector, all located in the Visakhapatnam City, Ferro Alloys Corporation, Shreeramnagar, Nellimerla Jute Mills Ltd., Nellimerla, Andhra Pradesh Paper Mills Ltd., Rajahmundry and Sri Ramadas Motor Transport Ltd., Kakinada were from the Private Sector. Visakhapatnam Port Trust and Dock Labour Board have more unskilled workers; while Ferro Alloys Corporation and Bharat Heavy Plate & Vessels were having more skilled personnel. A.P.P.M. and NJM have relatively balanced ratio of skilled and unskilled personnel. On the other hand, the three Public Sector Units consisted urbanised labour while the four Private Sector Units consisted workers with relatively more rural background.

During the study, the researcher conducted survey of the Unit Level Classes and met workers, Worker Teachers , trade union leaders, managements and education officers to administer questionnaires. Further, secondary data such as earlier publications, statistics of various agencies etc. have been utilised where it was necessary.

The selection of the sample for the present study was based on the availability of workers, Worker Teachers , trade union representatives and managements. The sample for the data consisted of three education officers, 85 Worker Teachers , 98 trained workers and 13 trade union representatives.

Majority of the Worker Teachers and workers were in the age-groups of 26-45 years and with a good service in the industry. Mostly they hailed from rural areas and caste groups belonged to SC/ST/BC. Experienced Worker Teachers were not in considerable number.

Very few of the Worker Teachers and workers were having educational qualifications beyond higher secondary/intermediate level. The difference in the levels of education of workers teachers and workers was very narrow. However, there were no illiterates or neo-literates in the Worker Teachers group. Perhaps because of this low levels of education, the motivation required to make them join the programme or even to make them respond to the present study has been difficult.

The response for the present study was 41.26% from Worker Teachers and 18.15% from the worker trainees, while it was only from the trade union representatives. On one hand, all the groups (Management, Trade Unions, Worker Teachers and Workers) have some degree of faith in the benefits of the Workers' Education Programme. However, in practice their participation has been different, for which the reasons attributed by them were discussed in detail. On the other, their interest in the Programme as can be seen from their regularity and activeness, was not upto the mark. More than 1/3rd of the Worker Teachers were inactive and not handling the classes. Such inactive Worker Teachers were relatively more in the public sector; and/or belonged to the age groups of 26-45. In one of the public sector industries, BHPV and one of the private sector industries (SRMT), the Programme was absolutely silent. 84.21% of the inactive Worker Teachers belonged to public sector undertakings. Only 12.94% of the Worker Teachers were conducting classes round the year (3 batches).

Nearly 2/3rds of the Worker Teachers have expressed that attendance in their classes was very poor and highly irregular. 67.35% of worker trainees expressed that domestic responsibilities and unsuitable timings were the common reasons for their irregularity.

Majority of the Worker Teachers have joined the programme on their own while nearly 80% of the worker trainees have joined after being motivated by their trade union leaders or Worker Teachers or managements etc. Of these, motivation by Worker Teachers was very high. Since most of the worker trainees have joined the programme upon the influence of others, their will, perhaps must be resulting in lack of interest in the programmes.

The topics favoured by Worker Teachers and worker trainees were mostly common. Only few people preferred to have vital subjects like industrial relations, safety, productivity, family planning etc.

The methods preferred for teaching includes discussions, seminars, lectures, debates, role plays and audio-visual teaching. However, most of the Worker Teachers were not having sufficient finances to adopt all these and organise or not being provided with the teaching aids.

It appears that teaching aids being provided to the Worker Teachers were not uniform to all the Worker Teachers , and other factors like the affiliation of the Worker Teachers to union and the worker teacher status in the union etc. Thus, contributing to the dissatisfaction among Worker Teachers and among workers it is causing severe disencouragement adding to their tiresomeness and domestic problems, further, the conditions in the class room were also very poor.

It appears that, most of the Worker Teachers were not successful in impressing their worker trainees to participate in various activities of learning. Less than 1/4th of the worker trainees were found to have participating in different activities of Unit Level Classes.

As expressed by the Worker Teachers and worker trainees, the co-operation of the management in promoting the facilities and the co-operation of CBWE in supervising and guiding the programmes, was not satisfactory. They complain of lack of adequate reading material; facility for a reading room and persons to guide them from time to time.

Further, 1/3rd of the worker trainees were not satisfied with the performance of their Worker Teachers. Incidentally, a majority of these worker trainees belonged to forward communities with urban background. The cognition attitude of different people at their work place, towards worker trainees was poor as expressed by nearly 30% of the worker trainees.

Results of the present study indicated problems of punctuality, wastage of time, increased resistance of Trade Unions, disciplinary actions etc. have eroded the work-discipline and some of the industries and the managements were of the opinion that Workers' Education Programme did not help in improving the situation.

Active involvement of some of the Worker Teachers in Trade Unions, politics and various other activities within the industries suggested that Workers' Education Programme helped in developing leadership qualities at least at the level of Worker Teachers . This is also evident from the fact that most of the Trade Unions referred in the present study were led by their own members.

An analysis of the results of the present study reveals that the participation of the managements or employers in the conduct of Workers' Education Programme is not as effective as required in extending their co-operation.

Perhaps because of all these lacunae in the conduct of ULCs, 42.35% of the Worker Teachers and 79.59% of the worker trainees were not having personal satisfaction for being involved in the programme. Even the trade union representatives also were not happy with the way of functioning of the Workers' Education Programme in their unions and 69.24% of them have expressed that the co-operation they extended to the Worker Teachers and worker trainees, was not upto the mark, for which they claim that financial constraints and low-key co-operation from the management and the CBWE were responsible.

For the successful completion of the programme, the Worker Teachers suggest that the co-operation from the managements and CBWE should be more by providing finances, facilities and congenial atmosphere. They recommended a legislative provision for having a special time-off to prepare themselves and train the workers, in addition to an increased honorarium and special incentives for those who actually conducts the programmes. They also suggested to make the Workers' Education Programme compulsory, by linking up with their career advancement through legislative measures. Similar types of suggestions were also made by the worker trainees. The suggestion of providing special incentives or increments to the Worker Teachers and worker trainees was also supported by the trade union representatives. They also wanted the Government through CBWE to meet the entire costs of running the programme to relieve their dependency even partial dependency, on the managements.

The analysis of the information on the income ranges of the workers in relation to their salary savings and debts accumulation, it appears that the plight of workers was not much different in their family economy, in spite of their education they had in the programme.

Similarly, the information on their utilisation of various leaves available to them indicated that their priority to duties at work place also showed little improvement after they had the training. Their conscious for family planning showed slight improvement. However, 58.33% of the fathers with more than 3 children (34) had their last issue after they had the training. On the whole, it can be summarised that the impact of training was far from realising the objective No.3 of the CBWE as considerable number of trainees were not able to plan their family economics, not improved their time planning for duties, not able to plan their family budget.

The opinion of Worker Teachers on the scope and relevance of the syllabi and training in ULC, to realise the seven objectives of the CBWE was analysed. The opinion was negative by 21.86% and minimal by 43.41%. 55.29% of the Worker Teachers indicates that the syllabus was not sufficient. Similar opinion of the trade union representatives also was collected in which 20.80% of negativity and 29.2% of minimal impact were recorded. The cumulative opinion of these two groups showed that 21.73% have opined negatively while 41.53% viewed minimal impact.

The trade unions like INTUC, AITUC and HMS, in spite of their dominance, size and network, could not yet mobilise their resources and are depending upon the grants-in-aid. Thus, a mechanism is to be evolved to ensure the trade unions, at least phase-wise in two plan periods or three plan periods, may establish and procure all necessities, to implement the Workers' Education Programme without any financial constraints. Only then the 7th objective of the CBWE, "to enable the trade unions to take over the Workers' Education Programme" can be realised.

Resolving this problem will also help into effectively implement the Workers' Education Programme and thereby to achieve the desired results. Based on the observations in the present study, few suggestions were made which may help in the improvement of the Programme.

(i) Proper legislations should be made to make the Workers' Education compulsory during the 1st year of service in any industry and senior Worker Teachers (based on their qualifications prescribed) are to be employed exclusively for the purpose, who will be continuously organising the programmes for the untrained workers.

(ii) The managements should link the programme with the career advancement of the workers and provide at least one additional increment to those who have successfully undergone the training.

(iii) It is also desirable to have at least an objective type test after the completion of each ULC batch.

(iv) The trade unions should co-ordinate with the managements to develop work discipline through Workers' Education and thereby contribute to the better industrial relations and healthy productivity.

(v) The course duration is to be extended from 3 months to 6 months with suitable revisions in the syllabi,

emphasizing work – discipline, collective bargaining, co-operatives, environment, occupational health and safety, etc.

(vi) The CBWE and the managements should co-operate in developing high use of audio-visual aids for effective teaching and also improve the class-room conditions.

(vii) Involvement of Universities and Institutions dealing with Labour Education is a must for better orientation.

Active research on various aspects of Workers' Education Programme is highly essential. To make a comprehensive review of the programme, the information from a majority of CBWE regions are much awaited. It is in the interest of the Nation that such studies in various regions should be initiated simultaneously. So far, a dozen good studies were available which evaluated or assessed or reviewed the Workers' Education Programme at regional or local levels. However, all have adopted different approaches in selecting the parameters to diagnose. The picture one can draw from it would be same as the seven metaphoric blindmen" description of an elephant. Thus, it is highly essential that urgent research is to be carried out to standardise the approach and methods to be adopted for evaluation and assessment of the programmes. This can be achieved by a seminary on the methods of assessment of the impact of Workers' Education Programme. This type of research can make the assessments scientific and systematic, so that a detailed comprehensive assessment of the programme at the National Level can be made which would help in improving the programme and realising the desired results at a faster pace than expected.

INDEX